Having   **Only**   **Positive**   **Expectations**

When You Need It Most

Col. 1:27

David O. Dykes

N·COURAGE
Resources

For a complete list of resources and broadcast messages by Dr. David O. Dykes, visit:
www.gabc.org

Green Acres Baptist Church
1607 Troup Highway
Tyler, Texas 75701
www.gabc.org

Produced with the assistance of Fluency Organization, Inc. in Tyler, TX. Cover design by DK Designs Group.

By David O. Dykes:

Jesus Storyteller: Timeless Truths from
His Parables
Revelation: God's Final Word
No, That's Not in the Bible

ALSO BY DAVID O. DYKES:

Finding Peace in Your Pain
Angels Really Do Exist: Signs of Heaven on
Earth
Ten Requirements for America's Survival
Character Out of Chaos
Handling Life's Disappointments
Do Angels Really Exist?

Available for download on your favorite e-reader.

Table of Contents

Introduction

*"We have this hope as an anchor
for the soul, firm and secure. It
enters the inner sanctuary behind
the curtain, where Jesus, who
went before us, has entered on our
behalf..." Hebrews 6:19-20*

In ancient times, an anchor was usually a rock with a hole in the middle large enough for sailors to pass a rope through it. Anchors weren't just used to keep a boat from drifting. Because seafaring was not an exact science as it is today, larger ships often had trouble entering a small harbor.

Sometimes the main ship paused outside the harbor entrance and placed its anchor in a smaller boat called a forerunner. The forerunner crew rowed the anchor into the harbor and dropped it in a safe location. Then the anchor line, attached to a pulley on the main ship was tightened so that the anchor would actually pull the ship safely into the harbor.

That's exactly the picture the writer of Hebrews paints about HOPE. Inside the Temple in Jerusalem, a thick curtain separated the Jews from the Holy of Holies, where God's earthly presence was located. When Jesus was crucified, that same curtain ripped apart to symbolize that every person now has access to God.

Jesus rose from the dead and is alive forevermore. He is our anchor, firmly rooted in God's presence in heaven. We are like the ship still out in the harbor, and He is our forerunner. We are attached to Jesus by a lifeline of faith. A "lifeline" is not that crease in the palm of your hand. A "lifeline" is not a phone call you make on a television quiz show. A lifeline is our faith connection with Jesus Christ. Sure, there are waves and storms in our earthly lives, but there is safety and security in heaven's harbor. Our only job is to hang onto the Anchor of HOPE, and He will see us all the way home.

Having   **Only**   **Positive**   **Expectations**

When My Heart Is Breaking

1

Everybody has had a broken heart. A newspaper in Nashville once decided to feature a series of articles on how different people deal with heartbreak. To get some ideas for stories, they wrote to several pastors and asked them to submit the names of people they knew who had gone through difficulty. One perceptive pastor mailed the newspaper a copy of the Nashville telephone directory! **At one time or another, everyone goes through heartache.**

From the cradle to the grave, pain comes our way like waves on the ocean. If your heart is not breaking over some loss, disappointment or tragedy right now, you're probably just between waves. Be thankful for the time-out and take a deep breath, but chances are good that another wave is on the way. That's life. No one is immune from the sharp-edged pain of a broken heart because the Bible says no one is immune from trouble. The Psalmist observed, "The length of our days is seventy years—or eighty, if we have the strength; yet their span is but trouble and sorrow, for they quickly pass, and we fly away." (Psalm 90:10)

Having Only Positive Expectations

Some people lose their appetite whenever they are hurting (while some hit the ice cream full force!). Some people lose sleep. Others lose the desire to go out and socialize with their friends and family. Some people lose their jobs because they are too depressed to get out of bed. At some point, some may even lose the desire to live. Of everything we stand to lose when we are hurting, the worst kind of heartache is when we begin to lose HOPE. Losing HOPE can literally make you sick, which is exactly what the Bible says in Proverbs 13:12, "Hope deferred makes the heart sick, but a longing fulfilled is the tree of life."

The Bible is full of stories about people who know something about losing HOPE. On the very first Easter, there were two heartbroken people walking from Jerusalem to their home in Emmaus. If you had been following these two friends, you'd have noticed their heads were hanging low and their feet were dragging. They were weighed down with a heavy load of discouragement and unbelievable disappointment. They had been followers of Jesus Christ, and just three days earlier they had seen their hopes and dreams nailed to a cross when Jesus was crucified by Roman soldiers. His arrest and violent death at the hand of His enemies was so unexpected—they never dreamed something this terrible could happen to someone they loved.

As they were walking along, a stranger joined them. They probably didn't feel like making small talk, but he asked them what had been going on in Jerusalem. The two friends stopped in their tracks—the Bible says they stood still, their faces downcast, as if it were too painful to talk about. They assumed this man had to be a visitor since he seemed so clueless about everything that had happened. So, they filled him in on who Jesus was and told him about Jesus being crucified.

Not only that, they told the stranger, things had gone from bad to worse after he died. Now his body was missing and there were all kinds of stories floating around about what had happened to him. They didn't know what to believe anymore.

As it turns out, this stranger knew a lot more about the Old Testament prophecies regarding the Messiah than they realized. He didn't seem at all bothered about what they were saying and started rattling off reasons why the Messiah *had* to die.

I imagine these two friends, overwhelmed by grief, were kind of listening half-heartedly at first as the stranger talked. However, he got their attention when he explained that every book in the Old Testament predicted how the Messiah would die at just the right time.

When they reached their home in Emmaus, the two disciples invited their guest to join them for supper and keep the conversation going. The man accepted their offer and came inside. When he picked up the bread to serve it, he said a blessing, which wasn't unusual. But this familiar mealtime tradition suddenly made them realize that the stranger was no stranger at all! It was the resurrected Jesus Himself. There must have been something about His appearance that kept them from recognizing Him before. At that split second, before they could say another word, "poof"—Jesus vanished.

But everything had now changed.

2

These two men knew what it was like to have broken hearts and shattered hopes. What's more, they were people of faith! How could this happen to them? Whenever I read this passage, a phrase they used when they were describing what happened to Jesus always stands out.

They said, "**We had hoped** that he was the one..." Life rarely turns out the way we planned does it? Have you ever looked at "what is" and mourned over "what could have been"? If you've ever felt that life delivered a big sucker punch in place of your dreams, you know how these two guys were feeling. Maybe you thought you'd have more money by this point in your life. Or maybe you hoped you'd be more successful at work. Maybe you thought you'd have kids by now.

How would you fill in the blank: "But I had hoped that…"? Maybe you're single and thinking, "But I had hoped to be married by now." Or you're divorced but you'd really hoped to stay married the rest of your life. You may be a student who hoped your parents wouldn't split up like all your other friends' parents. Remember, you're not the only one who has looked at how their lives turned out and said, "But I had hoped..."

I remember sitting in the hospital with my dad who was dying of cancer. He was a heavy smoker and cancer had metastasized into his lungs and brain. It was obvious to us that barring a miracle he was going to die. He was only in his mid-50s and I was not even thirty years old yet.

As the two of us were visiting together, we passed the time making small talk. Although it was hard for him to speak, I could tell he wanted to tell me something more important. Suddenly he looked at me and said, "Son, I had hoped..." He took another labored breath. "I had hoped...that when I retired, your mother and I would do some traveling. I realize now that I've made a mistake." My dad worked hard all of his life. Because of his job, we didn't have a lot of "real" vacations when I was growing up. Our vacations consisted of packing up the car for a weekend visit to my relatives. Sometimes for a special treat we spent a whole week during the summer visiting, you guessed it, more relatives.

He looked out the window of his hospital room, turned back to me and said with a seriousness I recognized from all the times I was in trouble as a child (and that was a lot of the time), "Don't you make the same mistake with your family. Don't wait until you retire to make some memories." Within a month, he was dead.

Everyone knows what it's like to wish our lives had taken a different turn. It's enough to make us want to throw up our hands and say, "What's the point anyway?" Thankfully, that's just about the time that God shows up and moves us in a new direction full of HOPE.

Having Only Positive Expectations

3

Several years ago when I was in China, God gave me a good acrostic for the word "HOPE." I have traveled to China a number of times because of a partnership our church has with a city there. In China, young people always enjoy practicing their English on English-speaking visitors. Many of the university students even give themselves English-sounding names.

I remember on one trip to China I met a Chinese student whose English name was Hope. I asked her if she knew the meaning of the English word "hope." To my surprise, she shook her head no. I smiled and said without even thinking, "The letters H-O-P-E stand for: Having Only Positive Expectations." She smiled back and repeated what I said. I'd never heard of or even thought about that acrostic before our conversation. I realized immediately that God gave it to me in that moment, and I don't think I'll come across a better definition for the word! Hope lived up to her name, too. That day she asked me for a Bible, which I gladly gave her. In the process of studying the Bible over the years, she has since become a tremendous believer who has a heart to lead her family and friends to Christ in China.

Having the kind of HOPE that Has Only Positive
Expectations can do amazing things. Sometimes we feel
as if we're at the end of our rope. HOPE can tie a
knot and encourage us to hold on. When
we look at the worst situation and Have Only Positive
Expectations for how it's going to turn out, we are
acknowledging our dependence on God to do what only
He can do.

When our two friends in Emmaus recognized Jesus
standing in their home, it ignited a spark in their cold
hearts again. In fact, they said, "Were not our hearts
burning within us as he talked with us on the road?"
(v32). Instead of thinking everything was lost, they
suddenly had a reason to believe things were not as bad
as they seemed. That's what HOPE does—it changes
our perspective in an instant. They didn't know exactly
what was going to happen or how Jesus was going to
fix the situation, but they rushed back to the rest of the
mourning disciples in Jerusalem to tell them things were
definitely beginning to look up!

In 1997, there was a movie starring Kevin Costner called
"The Postman." Hollywood movie critics ridiculed
it as one of the worst movies ever produced. That's
probably why I liked it. The movie is set in the future
after a terrible war completely destroys America and our
government. There are no jobs, no banks and no grocery

stores. Millions of people are financially devastated and homeless. Evil General Valentine is now in control and the star, Kevin Costner, is hiding out in an old wrecked Postal truck. He borrows the uniform off the skeleton of the poor former postman and wanders into an isolated town claiming to be a postman for the Reformed United States Government.

Hoping the people will take him in and feed him, Costner elaborates on his tale and tells the bewildered crowd that there's a new president named Richard Starkey (for you trivia nuts, that's Ringo Starr's real name). The President, he says, is living at the new U.S. Capital in Minneapolis and he sent the Postman with an important message that "stuff is getting better." To his amazement, they believe him.

The Postman is just a charlatan, but in the process his motives begin to change when he realizes how much he is encouraging these people—so much so that they eventually enlist a larger group of Postmen to lead a rebellion against General Valentine.

There's a scene in the movie where Abby, played by Olivia Williams, is talking about the power of HOPE. She says to Costner, "You have a gift, Postman…You've given us all back what we've forgotten…You give out hope like it was candy in your pocket."

When I heard that line, I thought, "That's exactly

what Jesus does." **Jesus gives out HOPE to everyone who encounters Him.** In fact, that's how he described His own mission on earth when He said, "[God] has sent me to heal the brokenhearted." (Luke 4:18 NKJV)

Has your heart been broken? Have you experienced such pain and disappointment that you've wondered, "What's the use?" Jesus is willing and able to heal your broken heart, but you must be willing to give Him all the pieces.

4

I once read a story about the end of WWII when a damaged submarine was limping back to dock at Newport News, Virginia. As it approached, something went wrong with the ballast system and it began to sink. When it came to rest on the bottom of the harbor, divers immediately began a rescue operation. As they reached the hull, they heard a loud, rhythmic tapping from one of the crewmembers inside. Someone was tapping in Morse code these solemn words: "Is…There… Any… Hope?" When we are in our darkest moment, that's what we most want to know: Am I going to make it? Is there any HOPE for me?

In this passage about the two friends walking with Jesus on the way to Emmaus, the phrase "walk with" speaks of a close relationship. Sometimes we refer to a person's "walk with God." It doesn't mean you log 10,000 steps on your pedometer every day with God. However, every day we face temptations suggesting that we walk down the wrong pathway in life. The Bible says, "Walk in the Spirit, and you will not fulfill the lusts of the flesh." (Galatians 5:16) In other words, when you're walking with God and connecting with Him in your everyday life by spending time with Him, He will direct you in the right pathway. The Bible also says, "Whether you turn to the right or to the left, your ears will hear a voice behind you say, 'this is the way, walk in it.'" (Isaiah 30:21) There is HOPE for you if you will walk with Christ.

Think about it. At the very moment that the two disciples were mourning their loss, Jesus was walking right beside them! Walking with Jesus means you acknowledge Him as your constant companion—in good times and bad. Sadly, many people who claim to be a Christian treat Jesus much the same way they treat their spare tire in the truck. Do you think about the Lord only when you have a personal "blow out?" Some people intellectually acknowledge that Jesus is always there, but they never really talk to Him until they have some kind of crisis and really need His help. If you want to have and maintain HOPE, you've got to walk with Him daily through prayer and reading His Word.

Not only did the two disciples on the road to Emmaus walk with Jesus, they listened to what He had to say. He started at Genesis and traced the Messiah's presence through every section of the Old Testament. They were shattered until they began to hear and pay attention to what He had to say.

If you're feeling hopeless, the Lord is trying to talk to you. Are you hearing His voice?

Having Only Positive Expectations

God's original intent for the world was to create people with whom He could have a personal, loving relationship. The Bible says He used to walk with Adam and Eve in the Garden of Eden. Sin destroyed that relationship, but salvation is a means to having that relationship restored. Through Jesus Christ, it's possible to know God and to walk and talk with Him. There is HOPE for you if you will listen to Him.

Having Only Positive Expectations

5

The two disciples walked with Jesus, they listened to Jesus, but it wasn't until He broke bread and blessed it that their eyes were fully opened. Something about that act revealed His true identity. Instead of dragging their feet the seven miles back to Jerusalem, they flew out the door at once to tell the other disciples the good news.

There is HOPE for you if you will see Christ for who He really is. Who is Jesus to you? If your answer is something like He was a religious teacher who lived and died 2,000 years ago, you wouldn't be wrong, but you wouldn't be completely correct either. He is so much more than the founder of a religion. If you have enough money or air miles, you can visit the tombs where the remains of all the religious leaders of all the religions of the world are buried. What makes Jesus unique is that He is still alive today. Easter is the most HOPE-full day of the year for Christians, but every day is Easter when you believe in Christ. The resurrection of Jesus is the basis for our HOPE—without it we really are HOPEless. "In his great mercy he has given us new birth into a living hope through the resurrection of Jesus Christ from the dead." (1 Peter 1:3) Some people have said that HOPE is the feeling you have that the feeling you have won't last forever. If you know Christ, you may go through some painful experiences in life, but your pain won't last forever. Tragedy will strike and you may feel as if your heart is breaking in a million pieces, but He can still hold you together.

Tale of a Broken Heart

I received an email many years ago from a single mom with two boys, ages six and eleven, who attended one of our Easter services. She gave me permission to share a portion of her letter, and I've never forgotten what she wrote:

> Last Sunday I saw that the weather was bad and there were so many people that twice I almost turned around. I also thought it would be the typical Easter service that you hear year after year. But I felt your message in a very personal way because I have suffered a severely broken heart.

> My husband died in October, so we have been trying to put the pieces of our lives together ever since. It has been a most difficult last two years. My husband was diagnosed with cancer and went on to suffer unimaginable pain, surgeries, chemo, radiation and finally total

disability, before his death.

...To say that my heart is broken is an understatement. However, I must force a smile and go on, because I have two boys that are counting on me. Every Sunday I feel so isolated, because now there is just one where there were two. This Sunday your service helped me not feel so alone.

...There are some days that you can imagine that it is a great struggle to put one foot in front of the other. I lost my best friend, my soul mate, and the father of my children. He did not live to see his boys grow to be young men or any future grandchildren. The losses are endless. I used to look down the road and see our future. Now I look and see a big blank...

Have you been there? Are you there now? This young single mom was slowly learning that Jesus is her only source of real HOPE. She went on to say that the HOPE she received through hearing God's Word at church was sometimes all she had to hang onto.

Life is full of unwanted an unexpected heartache. Walking with Jesus is the only way you can face heartache and still Have Only Positive Expectations about an unknown future. The best verse in the Bible that describes what it means to have real HOPE is

Having Only Positive Expectations

Romans 8:28: "And we know that in all things God works for the good of those who love him, who have been called according to his purpose."

If you build your life on the shifting sands of circumstances, you'll be in trouble. But if you turn your life over to Jesus, you can find HOPE— and a solid place to stand when the storms of life come crashing around you.

Having   Only   Positive   Expectations

When I've Messed Up

6

Melanie never was without a date. By the time she was old enough to get married, proposals were streaming her way. When Melanie met Ray, she was sure they would marry and live happily ever after. But she was wrong. After three years, the marriage was a disaster and divorce soon followed. Melanie was determined not to make the same mistake again, so when Robert came into her life she was careful. Robert was more levelheaded than Ray, and he promised her the world. So, Melanie walked down the aisle again. Within a year, that marriage was over, too.

Then sweet, fun-loving Reggie came along. Ray and Robert were boring, and Melanie knew she needed someone fun for a change. So, she and Reggie flew off to Las Vegas and got married. Melanie's family and friends started taking bets on how long it would last. Sure enough, after 14 months, the fun was gone and so was Reggie. Fast-forward 10 years. By now, Melanie has gone through a total of five husbands and five divorces. She's only in her late 30s, but her face carries the tracks of thousands of tears and each wrinkle has its own story.

Having Only Positive Expectations

Her friends and family laugh if off and call her a big flirt, but they use other words when she isn't listening. One day a friend at work invites her to church. Scared out of her mind about what people will say, but desperate for help, Melanie shows up one Sunday morning.

Now, let's hit the pause button.

I made up this story, but it follows the plot of the story of Jesus and the Samaritan woman in John 4. Like Melanie, the Samaritan woman was a woman with a past. She had been married a number of times and was currently living with a man. One day she crossed paths with Jesus as she was drawing water from the town well. That's when Jesus offered to give her "living water" instead. Jesus intrigued her when He said to her, "Everyone who drinks this water will be thirsty again, but whoever drinks the water I give him will never thirst. Indeed, the water I give him will become in him a spring of water welling up to eternal life." (John 4:14)

But then things got really interesting. He asked about her husband.

> The woman said to him, "Sir, give me this water so that I won't get thirsty and have to keep coming here to draw water."

> He told her, "Go, call your husband and come back."

Having Only Positive Expectations

"I have no husband," she replied.

Jesus said to her, "You are right when you say you have no husband. The fact is, you have had five husbands, and the man you now have is not your husband. What you have just said is quite true." (John 4:15-18)

In 1647, the Italian painter named Guercino (a nickname that meant "squinter") completed a painting of Jesus and the Samaritan Woman. In it, he captures this poignant moment in the story. In his painting, the woman is staring off into space with an expression that reveals her mixed emotions—regret for her mistakes and a longing for HOPE.

Her story and Melanie's story is a pattern of failure, disappointment and never-ending guilt. Is there HOPE after you fail? After you've royally messed things up, is everything over? Jesus told this true story as a reminder of a powerful truth. No matter what you have done, there is still HOPE for you.

Having Only Positive Expectations

Having Only Positive Expectations

7

When I started thinking about a biblical character I could use to write about HOPE when you've messed up, I found the choices were almost unlimited. Everybody in the Bible, except the Lord Jesus, sinned at one time or another. We tend to think of Bible characters as if they were super humans. But they struggled with failure the same way we do today. In fact, that's why their stories are in the Bible: for us to learn from their mistakes. Don't believe it? Check out Hebrews 11—it reads like the "Who's Who" from the Old Testament, and every one of them had skeletons in their closets.

This chapter is often called the "Roll Call of Faith." However, when you examine the list, you realize it just as easily could be called the Roll Call of Failures! For instance, Noah built the ark, but he also got drunk, stripped off his clothes and exposed himself. Abraham was the Father of the Faithful, but he also lied about Sarah being his wife when they visited Egypt. Isaac caused some major family drama when he blessed the wrong son. Jacob, whose name means "grabber," stole the birthright out from under his brother Esau. Moses, who delivered God's Ten Commandments, was also a cold-blooded murderer. Rahab is listed in Hebrews 11, but she was a prostitute. Samson was a he-man with a she-problem. And even David, a man after God's own heart, stole a man's wife, committed adultery and had her husband killed.

The list goes on.

The Bible reminds us that we have all sinned and fallen short of God's standard of perfection. (Romans 3:23) **Failure is a part of life.** But just because you fail, it doesn't mean *you're* a failure. Someone has noted the difference between failing and being a failure:

> Failure is not failing to reach your dreams.
> Failure is not having a dream.
> Failure is not setting a goal and missing it.
> Failure is not having a goal.
> Failure is not falling down. Failure is refusing to get back up.

The woman at the well didn't know it, but her scandalous failures were the very reason why Jesus wanted to talk to her. So many times we think God doesn't want anything to do with us because of our mistakes. We think we must clean up our own act before we can come to Him. However, Jesus said to the religious professionals of His day, "I have not come to call the righteous, but sinners to repentance." (Luke 5:32)

Although she probably thought she'd done a pretty good job of changing the subject when things got too personal, Jesus already knew everything about her. She already had three strikes against her. First, she was a woman. Except for their wives and family members, men in ancient Israel didn't even speak to women because they were thought of as inferior creatures. A daily prayer of the Pharisees was, "God, I thank thee that I was not born a Gentile, a dog or a woman."

This woman was also a Samaritan, a group considered half-breed Jews because they had intermarried with the Assyrians twelve generations earlier. This story took place in what we now call the West Bank, which is Palestinian territory. The way the Palestinians and the Israelis regard each other today is exactly the way the Jews felt toward the Samaritans in Jesus' day.

Third, she was living in adultery with another man. In our culture, we usually say, "Three strikes and you're out!" However, Jesus loved her anyway.

I think one reason why movies like *Shrek* are so popular is because we all want to believe in the power of love to transform us. Fiona, a green ogre who is the love interest of another green ogre named Shrek, was once a beautiful princess who lost her beauty because she fell under a spell. However, Shrek loves her for who she is on the inside, not on the outside. And, in a way, his love makes her beautiful.

That's not just Hollywood—that's the real kind of love Jesus has for you. The Bible says, "Man looks at the outward appearance, but the Lord looks at the heart." (1 Samuel 16:7) But even when He looks past what's outside and into our hearts, we are still unlovely! We are sinful and selfish to the core, and it's not as though we *deserve* His love on any level. And yet, knowing everything about us inside and out, He loves us anyway. Like Shrek, it is His love that transforms us into something beautiful to behold. "God loves you!" the bumper sticker says. But don't miss the point. **God doesn't love you because you're valuable. You're valuable because God loves you.**

That's what Jesus proved to the woman at the well when He accepted her as she was, not as she "should" be. She was feeling pretty hopeless the day she came to the well to draw water, stuck in a destructive pattern with no way out. Even if she had wanted to change, she didn't have the power to pull it off for the long term. What she saw in Jesus that day was the opportunity to start over—this time, for real.

Having Only Positive Expectations

8

We live in a messed up world—no wonder we are messed up people! In Genesis 3, God said part of the ramifications of Adam and Eve's sin was that the ground would be "cursed." What did that mean? Before Adam and Eve sinned, there were no sharp thorns, entangling thistles or choking dust. There was no sickness or death. The animal that died so it could provide a covering for Adam and Eve with its skin was the first death in Paradise. Just as humanity is crying out for HOPE and salvation, so the physical Creation has longed for redemption since the day sin entered the world.

Have you ever wondered why we have some many natural disasters like hurricanes, earthquakes, tornadoes and volcanoes? **Creation itself is fallen, groaning for redemption.** "For the creation was subjected to frustration... in hope that the creation itself will be liberated from its bondage to decay and brought into the glorious freedom of the children of God. We know that the whole creation has been groaning as in the pains of childbirth right up to the present time." (Romans 8:20-22)

Having Only Positive Expectations

Creation isn't waiting for more environmentalists to save it or the next global warming summit. It's waiting for Jesus. The only HOPE for all of Creation is Jesus Christ. The world we live in will not get any better until Jesus returns to create a new heaven a new earth, as Revelation describes. That's why Creation is looking for that "blessed hope—the glorious appearing of our Great God and Savior, Jesus Christ." (Titus 2:13)

While we live in this fallen world, we have a choice. The woman at the well had a choice about what to do with her past, too. If you realize you have messed up, you can experience His forgiveness and start over like she did.

Admit it! When Jesus confronted the woman at the well with her sexual immorality, she didn't deny it. She didn't justify it. She agreed with Jesus. "Sir, I can tell you are a prophet," she said. (John 4:19) (He was actually a lot more than that—but I'll give her credit for realizing there was no use in trying to hide the truth from Him!)

Coming clean is not natural for us. Think about how Adam and Eve hid from God when they sinned and started the finger pointing. Human nature has been trying to defend our actions and justify our bad behavior ever since. We don't call it "wickedness… we call it "a weakness." Today, when married people have sex with someone other than their mate, they don't call it adultery. They call it "an affair." Instead of calling it "a lie," we call it "stretching the truth." Instead of calling profanity "blasphemy," we call it "colorful language."

The Bible takes a different approach. It says, "He who conceals his sins does not prosper, but whoever confesses and renounces them finds mercy." (Proverbs 28:13) When you confess your sin, you are not telling God something He doesn't know. You don't have to say, "Now, Lord, this is going to surprise You, but yesterday I looked at someone with lust in my heart." Do you think God says, "What? I can't believe you would do something like that!" That's *not* the way it works. God already *knows* where and when you've messed up. The word for "confess" is *homolegeo*, which means "to say the same thing." When you confess your sin, you are simply saying the same thing about your behavior that God says. You are agreeing with Him that it is sin.

Quit it! When people mess up, they usually beg for another chance. An employee who is caught being late for the third time in a week may plead not to lose his job. A wayward man may beg his wife not to leave him. We are all about getting a second chance. However, the woman at the well didn't need a second or third chance; she needed a new life. God wants to give you something much more valuable than a second chance. God wants to give you a changed heart. That's what repentance is. It means a "change of mind" that leads to a "change of behavior."

A few chapters later in John 8, we read about Jesus'

Having Only Positive Expectations

conversation with another messed up woman. She had been caught in adultery and the pious Jews wanted to stone her. Jesus said, "If any one of you is without sin, let him be the first to throw a stone at her." (John 8:7) When her accusers left, Jesus didn't reach out His hand, pull her up and say, "Hey, I'm going to give you a second chance." He gave her that and much more when He told her to "leave your life of sin." He essentially released her from the guilt of her past and commissioned her to go and live a new life instead.

God knows the only way we are going to be free from the pet sins in our life is to turn and leave them behind with the help of the Holy Spirit. With God's supernatural assistance (not by "trying harder"), it is possible for you to walk in a new direction and leave your old life behind. **There is HOPE for everyone who has messed up and made mistakes.** No matter what.

First, admit it. Then quit it. But that leads me to the third step we must take if we want to experience the benefits of His forgiveness—and it's the hardest thing of all. Forget it.

9

Are you with me so far? If you really want to take God up on His offer of restoring HOPE to you when you mess up, you have to admit your sin and be willing to turn away from it. But there is one more important step to take.

Forget it! Once you have confessed and repented of your sin, then you must accept God's forgiveness. That is the hardest step to take for many people: believing God has completely forgiven you. I think that's why God makes so many promises in the Bible that assure us of His forgiveness.

> "Though your sins are like scarlet, they shall be as white as snow; though they are red as crimson, they shall be like wool." (Isaiah 1:18)

> "As far as the east is from the west, so far has he removed our transgressions from us." (Psalm 103:12)

> "You hurl all our iniquities into the depths of the sea." (Micah 7:19)

Having Only Positive Expectations

"In your love you kept me from the pit of destruction; you have put all my sins behind your back." (Isaiah 37:22)

"I, even I, am he who blots out your transgressions, for my own sake, and remembers your sins no more." (Isaiah 43:25)

God's nature is to forgive and forget. Our trouble is that we can't forget. Once you have accepted God's forgiveness, you must also forgive yourself. The devil can't prevent God from forgiving you, but he can try to talk you out of accepting that gift. He tries to make us doubt we're forgiven. That's why the Bible calls him "the accuser of the brothers." (Revelation 12:10) Even when you've confessed and repented of your sin, the devil wants you to feel dirty.

People often ask, "How can I distinguish between the accusing of Satan and the conviction of the Holy Spirit?" When my wife calls me on the phone, I don't have to ask, "Who is this?" I recognize her voice because we talk all the time. In the same way, if you know the Lord intimately, you'll recognize His voice. The devil tries to condemn you with lingering guilt over something. **But the Holy Spirit convicts you so you will admit it, quit it and forget it.** The devil does not want you to work through this process, and he makes you feel like a hopeless cause that even God cannot forgive.

Don't let him do that to you.

Having Only Positive Expectations

If you have confessed and repented of a particular sin, then accept God's forgiveness and forgive yourself (1 John 1:9). **Forget your past mistakes and move on toward the future.**

If anyone had a reason to let guilt paralyze him into thinking all was hopeless, it was the Apostle Paul. Talk about a messed up life! He participated in the persecution and arrest of many Christians. He even consented when Stephen was stoned to death. Even after he met Christ Himself on the road to Damascus, he continued to struggle with sin. In Romans 7 Paul wrote, "The things I want to do, I don't do. And the very things I don't want to do, I find myself doing." Yet Paul knew what it was to be forgiven and to move on. He also wrote, "One thing I do: Forgetting what is behind and straining toward what is ahead, I press on toward the goal to win the prize for which God has called me heavenward in Christ Jesus." (Philippians 3:13-14)

On the night of March 12, 2005, Ashley Smith experienced every woman's worst nightmare. As she was entering her apartment at 2:00 in the morning, escaped prisoner Brian Nichols came up behind her and stuck a gun in her ribs. For seven hours, a man who had gunned down several people in the past few hours held her hostage. Nichols tied her up and told her he was probably going to have to kill her, too.

Over the next few hours, a miracle occurred.

Having Only Positive Expectations

When she started talking about God, he untied her, but kept his guns within reach. Then she asked him if she could read something. She opened her Bible and pastor Rick Warren's book, *The Purpose Driven Life*. She had been reading a section of Rick's book each day, seeking to draw closer to God. Over the next few hours, they talked about God and the Bible.

The next morning, he allowed her to leave to pick up her daughter from an AWANA event at a local Baptist church. She called 911 and when police surrounded her apartment, Nichols surrendered without any resistance.

I remember admiring Ashley Smith when I read her story. The national media revealed how she had gone through years of heartbreaking failures and disappointments. She'd been through drug and alcohol rehab and had even given up custody of her daughter. The reason she left her apartment in the middle of the night was to go buy cigarettes.

She didn't claim to be a person who has it all together, yet God was very near to her that night. She was simply in the process of getting it all together. That's what HOPE is. Even when life is bad, you're still looking to God and Having Only Positive Expectations. It's been said humans can live about 40 days without food, three days without water and about eight minutes without air—but not one second without HOPE. There was HOPE for someone like Nichols. Ashley knew that was true because God had not given up on her either!

Having Only Positive Expectations

Having   Only   Positive   Expectations

When I'm Afraid

10

There are over 500 fears registered with the American Medical Association as being legitimate phobias. They include such unusual fears as:

- Cyberphobia: fear of computers
- Lunaphobia: fear of the moon
- Astraphobia: fear of lightning
- Chrometophobia: fear of money
- Erytophobia: fear of the color red
- Triskaidekaphobia: fear of the number "13"
- Peladophobia: fear of baldness
- Phobophobia: fear of fear (yes, really)

But the most common fear among Americans is *glossophobia*, which is the fear of public speaking. About 20% of Americans report they have an irrational fear at the thought of standing up in front of a crowd and speaking. Comedian Jerry Seinfeld has said, "At a funeral, most people would rather in be in the casket than giving the eulogy."

There is actually a kind of fear that is good for you. In

some instances, fear is a God-given warning system. It's the fear of getting killed that makes you look both ways before you cross a busy street. It's the fear of getting bitten that causes you to stay away from a rattlesnake. Healthy fear releases adrenalin, which prepares you to flee or fight when danger is near.

But there is a damaging kind of fear that causes a person to freeze up like a deer caught in headlights. Julius Caesar was a powerful emperor, yet he was so afraid of thunder that he hid under his bed during storms! Peter the Great was a feared Russian Czar, yet he was so afraid of bridges that he refused to use them. **You may have irrational, harmful fears that keep you from enjoying life.** This kind of fear produces emotional paralysis.

So, the first thing to do with your fear is to determine if it is the healthy or unhealthy kind. **Once you face your fears and name them, you are on your way to conquering them.**

One of the reasons I love to read the Psalms is that there is a Psalm for every human emotion—including fear. In Psalm 55, King David gives a vivid description of being terribly afraid of what is going to happen to him. Saul is chasing him with the intent to kill him. He prayed:

> "Listen to my prayer, O God, do not ignore
> my plea; hear me and answer me. My thoughts

trouble me and I am distraught at the voice
of the enemy, at the stares of the wicked; for
they bring down suffering upon me and revile
me in their anger. My heart is in anguish
within me; the terrors of death assail me.
Fear and trembling have beset me; horror has
overwhelmed me." (55:1-5)

He goes on to describe how he is in danger, but then his
psalm takes a comforting turn with these simple words:

"But I call to God, and the Lord saves me." (55:16)

Even when you're trembling inside with fear, and you
don't know what is going to happen tomorrow, there is
HOPE today.

Having Only Positive Expectations

ꞌ

Having Only Positive Expectations

11

There are two words in the New Testament for fear. *Eulabeia* means "respect, or reverence." That is the word the Bible uses when it commands us to "fear the Lord." This is a different kind of fear that you can remember by the acrostic: F-E-A-R. The Father Earns our Awe and Respect. **God doesn't want you to be afraid of Him.** He wants you to respect how holy He is. An electrician has to maintain a healthy fear of electricity because he knows it can kill him. Yet, his fear of electricity doesn't prevent him from doing his job. In the same way, we can have a reverential fear of God that causes us to respect Him without cringing in terror.

The other word for fear in the New Testament is *phobeo*, which means a strangling, debilitating fear. That's where we get the word, "phobia." Thousands struggle with irrational panic attacks and unreasonable bouts of fear that cause them to live a life that is less than what God intended. God wants you to overcome any unhealthy fears that prevent you from living by faith.

Dr. E. Stanley Jones once wrote: "I am inwardly fashioned for faith, not for fear. I am so made that worry and anxiety are sand in the machinery of life; faith is the oil. In anxiety and worry, my being is gasping for breath—but in faith and hope, I breathe freely." Fear can strangle your soul and gum up your spirit.

I used to tell people that East Texas was the greatest place in America to live because of the beautiful scenery, the friendly people and the low crime rate. However, in recent years this feeling of security that we enjoyed for so long has been threatened.

There was a terrible abduction and murder at a large superstore and then a terrifying courthouse shooting. Before we could catch our breath, a troubled man entered a nearby high school and shot the head football coach. Evil is everywhere—even in East Texas. But God doesn't want us to live in constant fear.

One of things that was causing David problems was "the voice of the enemy... the stares of the wicked." (Psalm 55:3) He knew a thing or two about encountering wicked, mean people. When he was a teenager, he faced a nine-foot giant named Goliath. Before David went out to meet Goliath, Saul tried to dress him in his armor to protect him. The heavy armor was much too large for a boy like David, so he refused to wear it. Instead, he went out to face Goliath dressed in better armor. He was depending on God's strength. David told Goliath, "You come against me with a sword, and a spear, and a javelin, but I come against you in the name of the Lord Almighty." (1 Samuel 17:45)

You are going to face Goliath-sized fears throughout your life. However, don't be afraid. You can come against your fears in the name of the Lord God Almighty.

David gave the antidote for poisonous fear when he wrote, "Evening, morning, and noon I cry out in distress, and he hears my voice." (Psalm 55:17) David had the kind of relationship with God that he spoke to Him on a regular basis. When trouble came, God didn't have to say, "Now who are you again?" If you have a regular time of prayer, you'll find that your greatest fears will melt away. God is with you.

Jesus said, "I tell you my friends, do not be afraid of those who kill the body and after that can do no more... Fear him who, after the killing of the body, has power to throw you into hell... indeed, the very hairs of your head are numbered. Don't be afraid." (Luke 12:4-6)

Again, the fear of God simply means we respect Him. Oswald Chambers once wrote, "It is the most natural thing in the world to be scared, and the clearest evidence that God's grace is at work in our hearts is when we do not get into panics... The remarkable thing about fearing God is that when you fear God you fear nothing else, whereas if you do not fear God you fear everything else." Remember, enemy number one—the devil—knows God's name and he is terrified of him. Why then should you be afraid of him or what his wicked servants can do?

12

Many people fear the future. If you let your mind run away, you can start entertaining all kinds of thoughts about bad things that *could* happen. As you look toward the next couple of years, is there uneasiness in your spirit? That feeling didn't come from God.

The Bible says in 2 Timothy 1:7, "For God has not given us the sprit of fear, but of power, and of love and a sound mind." God is not the author of fear. The devil is the sinister minister of fear. He knows that if he can keep you in fear, you'll be ineffective as a Christian.

In Psalm 55:2, David complained, "My thoughts trouble me and I am distraught." That's where most of our fears originate—distressing thoughts that run through our minds over and over again.

"Cast your cares on the Lord and he will sustain you," David wrote in answer to this problem. (Psalm 55:22) Do you have worries or fears about your future? **Throw all your cares onto God's shoulders.** He can bear every one of your sorrows

Having Only Positive Expectations

and still have room for more. If you are a child of God, there's HOPE for your future.

Listen to God's promise: "For I know the plans I have for you I have for you," declares the Lord, "plans to prosper you and not to harm you, plans to give you HOPE and a future." (Jeremiah 29:11) You don't have to be afraid of what your future holds as long as you know who holds your future.

In Proverbs 31, we read about a noble woman who followed God's ways. She had an interesting perspective on the future. The Bible says, "She is clothed with strength and dignity; she can laugh at the days to come." (31:25) When you think about it, it is almost comical what lengths the devil will go to in order to make you worry. In light of the great God we have, we should never be afraid. When the devil makes you fearful, just laugh in his face and say, "Ha! God has a plan for me, and it is a plan to prosper me, not to harm me. It is a plan for HOPE and a future!"

Of course, the number one thing people fear about the future is dying. After all, the idea of dying can be pretty scary. One of my favorite stories is about the preacher who was preaching about being prepared to die one day. In a thunderous voice, he said, "Every member of this church is going to die!" At that, a kid on the front pew laughed out loud. Startled, the preacher repeated his statement a little louder. "I said, EVERY MEMBER

OF THIS CHURCH IS GOING TO DIE!" To his dismay, the kid laughed even louder. The preacher stopped and said, "Young man, how can you laugh at that?" The young boy replied, "Because I'm not a member of this church!"

In the 14th century, the Italian poet Dante Alighieri wrote a trilogy of books tracing his imaginary journey through hell, purgatory and then heaven. His first book is the most famous titled, *The Inferno*. In it, he described hell as seven circles of increasing punishment, based on the seven deadly sins. His descriptions are fictitious, but he does get one detail of hell correct: Hell is completely devoid of hope. In fact, Dante's inscription above the entrance to hell stated, "Through me the way into the city of woe…abandon all hope, you who enter here."

As Christians, death is not the end. That is why we have HOPE. Sure, we grieve at the death of loved ones, but we don't sorrow in the same way as those who have no HOPE (1 Thessalonians 4:13). As a pastor, I've often had the difficult assignment of preaching a funeral of someone who showed no evidence of being a follower of Jesus. The depth of sorrow and hopelessness at funerals like that is totally different than the funeral of someone who is a devoted follower of Jesus.

Bertrand Russell was one of the most influential thinkers of the 20th century. But Russell wasn't a

Christian. In 1927, he wrote a book entitled *Why I Am Not a Christian*. When he was eighty-one, he was interviewed by a BBC reporter who asked him, "What do you have to hang onto when death is obviously so close?" Russell's answer was: "I have nothing to hang onto but grim, unyielding despair."

The Bible says, "For, to me, to live is Christ and to die is gain." (Philippians 1:21) Life and death are win-win situations for a Christian. If we live, we experience the spiritual presence of Jesus in our day-to-day lives. If we die, it's *gain* because we'll be in the literal presence of Jesus!

There's a poignant scene in my favorite movie, *Forrest Gump*, when he goes over to his friend Jenny's house. Jenny's dad has been abusing her, so she grabs Forrest's hand and they run into the cornfield to hide. Jenny drags Forrest to his knees and says, "Pray with me Forrest. *Dear, God, make me a bird so I can fly far, far, far away from here.*" Have you ever felt that way? David did. He wrote about "the terrors of death" in Psalm 55 because he fully expected to die any day at the hand of his former friend. Fear had so consumed him that he wished he could have the wings of a dove to fly far way to a place of rest.

Fear triggers a fight or flight response, and we've discovered it's easier to flee than to fight. But because of God's love and grace, there's a better response beyond fight or flee; there is faith. And faith produces HOPE. HOPE is simply faith in the future tense!

Faith and fear cannot exist together. Feed your faith, and your fears will starve to death! Did you hear about the time fear knocked at the door? Faith answered. And guess what? No one was there!

Having Only Positive Expectations

Having Only Positive Expectations

Having   Only   Positive   Expectations

When I Feel Like Quitting

13

It's a joke in the South that all Baptist preachers love fried chicken. But I heard of one pastor who couldn't stand it. In fact, he hated fried chicken. One time this pastor was preaching a weeklong meeting at another church, and he was eating in the homes of members before the services. Every night, he was served the same meal (you guessed it): fried chicken. After five nights of fried chicken, he arrived at a home for the final meal of the week. There in front of him was a big platter of crispy, fried chicken. He could hardly look at it. To make matters worse, the host asked him to pray the blessing. So the preacher prayed this prayer: "Lord, I've had it hot and I've had it cold; I've had it young and I've had it old; I've had it tender, and I've had it tough, But, thank you, Lord, I've had enough!"

At one time or another, we want to throw in the towel and say, "I've had enough!" One of the greatest prophets of the Old Testament was Elijah. But in 1 Kings 19 we read about a time when he was so down that he was ready for God to take him home early! One of the most evil couples in the

Bible—King Ahab and his wife, Jezebel— were eager to help make that happen! Elijah and about 450 prophets of Baal had a God-contest on top of Mt. Carmel to determine which "god" reigned supreme. After God embarrassed the queen's prophets (and Elijah had them all slaughtered), she wanted Elijah dead.

> Now Ahab told Jezebel everything Elijah had done and how he had killed all the prophets with the sword. So Jezebel sent a messenger to Elijah to say, "May the gods deal with me, be it ever so severely, if by this time tomorrow I do not make your life like one of them."
>
> Elijah was afraid and ran for his life. When he came to Beersheba in Judah, he left his servant there, while he himself went a day's journey into the desert. He came to a broom tree, sat down under it and prayed that he might die. "I have had enough, Lord," he said. "Take my life; I am no better than my ancestors." Then he lay down under the tree and fell asleep."
> (1 Kings 19:1-4)

Try to imagine a young Billy Graham sitting under a solitary tree in the desert after one of his greatest crusades. Thousands of people just got saved and he thinks his life is over. Elijah had just had one of the greatest victories of his life on Mt. Carmel. God had sent down fire from heaven in answer to Elijah's prayers—

Having Only Positive Expectations

proving Elijah's authority to an entire kingdom. Also, a three-year drought had been broken. He should have been on top of the world, yet we find him in the depths of depression and begging God to let him die.

We sometimes think the Old Testament characters were superhuman, but they were just like us. And we are just like them. Many of us know what it's like to go from the mountaintop of happiness to the valley of despair. Stories like Elijah's are written to give us HOPE. Romans 15:4 says, "For everything that was written in the past was written to teach us, so that through endurance and the encouragement of the Scriptures we might have hope."

Have you ever heard the expression about going through problems, "It's enough to make a preacher cuss"? I heard a story about a pastor who stopped at a yard sale to buy a used lawnmower. There was a kid who was doing his best to make the sale. The preacher pulled the rope several times to crank the mower, but it wouldn't start. The boy said, "You have to kick it and say a few cuss words before it will crank." The preacher replied, "Son, I can't do that. It's been years since I used a cuss word." The kid said, "Just keep pullin' the rope and it'll come back to you."

It could be that you find yourself in the same place as Elijah. You've lost HOPE and you feel like quitting. Even committed followers of God

Having Only Positive Expectations

sometimes get discouraged. Elijah was ready to give up, but God wouldn't let him.

14

It's easy to see the reasons why Elijah wanted to quit. They're the same reasons that make people want to give up today.

We want to quit when we feel physically drained. Elijah was literally running for his life. He ran all the way from Jezreel to Beersheba, which is about 70 miles. He was already exhausted from his confrontation with the 450 prophets of Baal, and his sprint only exhausted him further.

Sometimes we work and work until we're exhausted, and then we grit our teeth and work a little longer. People's schedules are more hectic than ever before. Moms and dads are so busy they seldom have time for their kids, much less each other. One reason I don't believe in evolution is because if it were true, mothers would have four hands. When you are worn out, you are prone to discouragement that leads to depression.

We want to quit when we feel emotionally deserted. The wicked queen hated Elijah and was out to get him, for sure. However, Elijah exaggerated the situation and thought *everyone* was against him. Notice how in verses 10 and 14 of 1 Kings 19 he tells God that "he is the only one" still faithful. Elijah was having a pity party for one. When you are down, the devil often shoves you into fear and paranoia. Some people have become so paranoid they can't even attend a football game anymore because they're certain the guys in the huddle are talking about them!

We all have problems. Do you know the difference between a big problem and a small problem? A big problem is anything I'm going through and a small problem is anything you're going through! It's like minor surgery—it's never "minor" when you are the one having the surgery. If you isolate yourself from others, like Elijah did, you become an easy target for the devil's discouragement.

We want to quit when we are spiritually depleted. Elijah had just experienced a wonderful spiritual high on Mt. Carmel. Immediately after that, he was full of despair and depression. It's easy to go from the peak to the pit! Sometimes you can be so involved with serving the Lord that you find yourself running on empty. Something you once enjoyed in ministry can become drudgery. Don't be surprised if you find yourself sagging emotionally and spiritually after you've had a mountaintop experience with the Lord. It's common throughout the Bible. Watch out when you're drained physically, deserted emotionally and depleted spiritually because that's exactly the time you'll find yourself wanting to quit.

I saw a funny cartoon not long ago that communicated the value of persistence. The cartoon pictured a large bird standing in shallow water. The bird had caught a juicy frog and was in the process of eating it, but the frog was clutching the throat of the bird so the bird couldn't swallow him. The caption said, "Never give up."

An unknown author wrote this poem:

> When things go wrong, as they sometimes will,
> When the road you're walking seems all uphill,
> When funds are low and debts are high,
> When you try to smile but have to cry,
> When your cares are pressing you down a bit,
> Rest if you must, but don't you quit!

Instead of letting Elijah quit, God gave him some specific directions that restored his HOPE. If you've gone from the pinnacle to the pit, this same advice will serve you well.

Having Only Positive Expectations

Having Only Positive Expectations

15

I once read that a century ago Americans averaged more than nine hours sleep a night. Today the average is slightly less than seven hours a night. The legendary football coach Vince Lombardi said, "Fatigue makes cowards of us all." That's why I've never mind if people sleep during my message. When I see them snoozing, I think, "If that's the only time they get still enough that they can catch a nap, at least they got *something* out of my message!"

If you are facing a decision about your job, your marriage, your education—whatever it is—and all you can think about is how much you want to quit, pay attention to your body. When Elijah was in the critical zone of depression, God gave him three things we all need: food, sleep and exercise.

Then he lay down under the tree and fell asleep.

All at once an angel touched him and said, "Get up and eat." He looked around, and there by his head was a cake of bread baked over hot coals,

Having Only Positive Expectations

and a jar of water. He ate and drank and then
lay down again.

The angel of the Lord came back a second time
and touched him and said, "Get up and eat, for
the journey is too much for you." So he got up
and ate and drank. Strengthened by that food,
he traveled forty days and forty nights until he
reached Horeb, the mountain of God. There he
went into a cave and spent the night.
(1 Kings 19:5-9)

Elijah was so exhausted that he slept for two days. If
you aren't getting enough rest, then you develop what
experts call a sleep debt—and it's a debt that will
eventually need to be repaid. It may be paid by poor
performance or an emotional collapse, but catching up
on your sleep is the best option.

An angel also kept prompting Elijah to eat. When he
woke up the first time, the angel had prepared a cake
for him to eat. (What kind of cake? Angel food cake,
of course!) What we eat can affect how we feel—not
only physically but also emotionally. Getting the right
amount of nutrients and "good" food is crucial to
maintaining our health.

Then God made Elijah put on his track shoes and get in
an exercise program! He had him walk for 40 days to Mt.
Horeb in the Sinai Peninsula, probably averaging five

miles a day. It is well proven that people who exercise
on a regular basis have much fewer bouts of depression
and discouragement. The only way you can change your
life is to change something you do daily. After all, it's
not your body; it's His temple. **If you've got the
blahs, try paying more attention to your
body.**

After his eating and exercise program, Elijah arrived
at Mt. Horeb, which is the same place as Mt. Sinai in
Exodus. Here, as Elijah slept in a dark cave, God taught
him something about how to listen to Him.

> The Lord said, "Go out and stand on the
> mountain in the presence of the Lord."...After
> the wind, there was an earthquake, but the
> Lord was not in the earthquake. After the
> earthquake came a fire, but the Lord was not
> in the fire. And after the fire came a gentle
> whisper... "What are you doing here, Elijah?"
> (1 Kings 19:11-13)

God sent a tornado, then an earthquake and then a
fire to get Elijah's attention. Just imagine for a moment
you're Elijah in that dark cave. You're straining to hear
God speak, and suddenly you hear the sound of a
powerful wind blowing. But you can't hear God's voice
in the tornado. Then there is the rumble of a mighty
earthquake and the giant rocks around you split, but,
again, God is not yet speaking. Finally, there is a roaring

Having Only Positive Expectations

fire. You're trying to listen, but all you hear is the crackle and sizzle of the flames. After these three colossal demonstrations, you hear a whisper calling your name.

God wants to talk to you, but it could be that there is so much noise in your life that you can't hear His voice. **God is speaking softly and simply, are you listening?** God doesn't speak in an audible voice— He speaks to your heart. He communicates on the level of your spirit, not your ears. God speaks most clearly to us in His Word, the Bible. If you open your heart, God will communicate with you. He wants to speak words of HOPE into your troubled soul. In John 16:33 Jesus said, "I have told you these things, so that in me you may have peace. In this world you will have trouble. But take heart! I have overcome the world." HOPE doesn't deny the reality of pain. HOPE simply denies the finality of it!

16

I enjoyed the movie *Gladiator* starring Russell Crowe because I love Roman history (and I love a good guy-fight). Russell Crowe plays Maximus, a former military general now reduced to a slave. He becomes a gladiator, which was the WWF of Roman entertainment. In one scene, Maximus and his fellow gladiators enter the coliseum armed for battle. They look invincible. But then the doors open and about a dozen charioteers thunder into the coliseum, armed with weapons and shields. The chariots have razor sharp blades extending from the wheels. The gladiators are outnumbered and overmatched. There is a moment of panic, but Maximus says six words that are the key to victory. Just before the fight ensues, he says, "If we stay together, we survive." So instead of separating the gladiators to make them easy prey, the charioteers were forced to battle a tight knot of fighters who were protecting each other's backs.

That's good advice for Christians today. **Satan's plan is always to divide and conquer.** He wants to divide every marriage, every family, every church and every community. We read in 1 Peter that Satan is like a roaring lion. His strategy is to separate weak Christians from the safety of the herd and attack them. Our job is to stick together.

One of the biggest delusions of depression is to think you're all alone and no one understands. However, many people have struggled with exactly the same thing you're facing. And God's message to you is the same one He gave Elijah when he thought he was the only prophet still following God. God said, "I reserve seven thousand in Israel—all whose knees have not bowed down to Baal and whose mouths have not kissed him." (1 Kings 19:18) Elijah was far from alone.

The best place to find people to share your burdens is in church. The church is not a showcase for shiny saints; it is a hospital for suffering sinners. *Every* follower of Jesus needs to be a part of a local church. If you want to find HOPE, link up with others who can help you. Hollywood and MTV can easily out-glitz the church. We can never pull off the entertainment extravaganzas that they can offer. However, the church of the Lord Jesus Christ offers something today you can't find anywhere else: HOPE. **Every church that preaches Jesus offers HOPE.**

I recall the first time I drove from Tyler to Canton, Texas. I saw a sign on Texas Highway 64 that said, "Little Hope Baptist Church." I almost skidded off the road! I remember thinking, "What? That's a terrible name for a church!" I thought that they should call themselves

"New Hope" or at least "Some Hope." The only thing worse than "Little Hope" would be "No Hope Baptist Church."

But then I learned "the rest of the story." I contacted the pastor who told me that the community got its name from a little girl named Hope Moore who died in the 19th century. Her family donated land in her honor for a church, thus the name "Little Hope." But the sign is still puzzling, if you ask me. I wonder what kind of "sign" others see in our lives (and on our faces) when we're going through a tough time. **Are we moping around and acting as if we have little HOPE?** Or is our countenance hopeful, boldly trusting God?

Life is tough, even for those who follow the Lord, but your attitude makes all the difference. One of my favorite stories is about a farmer who owned an old mule that was almost blind. The farmer knew the mule should be put down, but he couldn't bring himself to do it. One day, the old mule accidentally fell in an abandoned well. The farmer heard the old mule braying and went to investigate.

The farmer determined that neither the old mule nor the old well was worth the trouble of saving. So, he enlisted some neighbors to fill in the well and bury the poor animal at the same time. When the first few shovels of dirt fell on him, the old mule became frantic. But then

Having Only Positive Expectations

he made a choice that saved his life. Instead of giving up and being buried alive, he decided that whenever dirt landed on him, he would simply shake it off and step on it. So, that's what he did. Shovel after shovel of dirt fell, "Shake it off, step on it. Shake it off, step on it." No matter how painful the blows, or distressing the situation, he wouldn't give up. He kept on shaking it off and stepping on top of it. Before long, the old mule stepped over the edge of the well—battered and bruised—but he was free. Life throws a lot of dirt on you sometimes. Are you going to quit? Or are you going to shake it off, step on it and be set free?

Having Only Positive Expectations

HOPE

Having   Only   Positive   Expectations

When My Family Is Falling Apart

17

Families remind me of the opening line in *A Tale of Two Cities* by Charles Dickens. "It was the best of times, it was the worst of times..." On one hand, our family members can be the greatest source of happiness in our lives. At the same time, family members can be the greatest source of pain and anguish. When you start looking in the Bible for a family that had problems, you don't have to look very far. You can open the Bible to almost any page and find stories about real people, in real families who were suffering real pain—just like families do today.

Most of us know the story of Joseph, and his coat of many colors. But sometimes we overlook what a sad, dysfunctional family he had. His father Jacob was the last of the big three of the Old Testament: Abraham, Isaac and Jacob. His relationship with his father is where Joseph's problems really began.

I've often thought that a fictional journey into Joseph's therapist's office would read like a soap opera. Imagine Joseph has just reclined on the couch and begins to tell his therapist about his family:

*"I guess it all started when my dad stole from Uncle Esau,
who then vowed to kill him. But my dad was always
scheming. When he first saw my mom, Rachel, he really
wanted to marry her. So my other granddad, Laban, made
Dad work for him seven years before they could marry. Then
on their wedding night, the schemer got snookered because
Grandad Laban smuggled Aunt Leah into Dad's bed
instead. Dad eventually ended up with two wives, as a result.
He loved my mom, but he didn't like Aunt Leah. Mom
became so angry after Leah started having his children that
she ordered Dad to stop sleeping with Leah. Then, since
Mom couldn't have children, she told Dad to have sex with
her maid. By now, the feud between Mom and Aunt Leah
had really heated up. Aunt Leah decided if Mom could do
it, she could do it, too. So, Aunt Leah gave her maid to Dad.
Before long, I had two more half-brothers.*

*"Finally, Mom got pregnant with me, but she died soon after
she gave birth to my little brother Benjamin. My dad was
never the same after that. He took the love he had for Mom
and directed it to Ben and me. That just made my other
brothers mad. I don't even have time to tell you about when
one of my stepsisters got raped. Or when one of my brothers
slept with one of Dad's wives, or how another brother slept
with his own daughter-in-law.*

*"The main problem is that all my older brothers hated me.
One day they beat me up and threw me into a pit. They*

Having Only Positive Expectations

*were going to kill me, but at the last minute they sold me as
a slave. That's how I ended up here in Egypt. Oh, I'm out of
time already? Thanks, Doc. Same time next week?"*

There's not much fun in a dysfunctional family.
If you have a messed up family, don't think you
are alone. If God could heal *that* family, He can heal your
fractured family, too.

A few years ago, my wife and I saw the movie "Hope
Floats" starring Sandra Bullock. Sandra Bullock's
character, Birdee Pruitt, married her high school
sweetheart and thought she would live happily ever
after. A few years later, while appearing on a talk show,
she learns her husband and best friend are having an
affair. After a messy divorce, Birdee and her daughter
Bernice move back to her small hometown to rebuild
their lives.

There is one scene in the movie that absolutely tore
out my heart and stomped it flat. Bernice's dad visits
Texas and Bernice decides she wants to go live with
him instead of her mother. The only problem is, her dad
doesn't really want her. As he drives off, Bernice is left
standing there crying with her little suitcase in hand. If
that doesn't break your heart, it's unbreakable.

The title from the movie comes from a line at the end
as Birdee and Bernice are beginning to think they will
survive. Birdee says, "Beginnings are scary. Endings are

Having Only Positive Expectations

usually sad, but it's what's in the middle that counts. So, when you find yourself at the beginning, just give hope a chance to float up and it will."

It's a good line, but HOPE doesn't just "float" up. **HOPE is an anchor.** Having Only Positive Expectations means you have something solid you can hang onto. The Bible says, "We take hold of the hope offered to us... We have this hope as an anchor for the soul, firm and secure. It enters the inner sanctuary behind the curtain, where Jesus, who went before us, has entered on our behalf." (Hebrews 6:18-20)

18

When it looks like we are down to nothing, God is up to something. If you're struggling with a lot of pain in your family life, you may be wondering where God is and what He's doing. **You may not realize it, but God is at work.**

Let's fast-forward about 30 years after the teenage Joseph was sold into slavery. The more familiar story is about how Joseph ends up as a servant in Potiphar's house and goes to prison unjustly. Then he gets out and becomes second-in-command to Pharaoh and saves the day when his family comes to Egypt looking for food during a global famine. However, that's not the end of the story. What happened next is not as well known, but it teaches a valuable lesson about family forgiveness.

By now, Jacob's family has moved to live with Joseph in Egypt. For his dad's sake, Joseph treated his conniving brothers with kindness. But some of the brothers must have feared the day when Jacob died, assuming they would be put to death for all the pain they'd caused Joseph decades earlier.

Having Only Positive Expectations

> When Joseph's brothers saw that their father
> was dead, they said, "What if Joseph holds
> a grudge against us and pays us back for all
> the wrongs we did to him?" So they sent
> word to Joseph saying, "Your father left these
> instructions before he died: 'This is what you
> are to say to Joseph: I ask you to forgive your
> brothers the sins they committed in treating
> you so badly.' Now please forgive the sins of the
> servants of the God of your father."
>
> When their message came to him, Joseph wept.
> (Genesis 50:15-17)

It broke Joseph's heart to realize his brothers had
been thinking all this time that the only reason he was
nice to them was because their dad was still living.
**Misunderstandings and mixed signals
are the mainstay among dysfunctional
families.**

The brothers did not realize that the entire time
Joseph was suffering at their hands, God was at work.
However, Joseph recognized this truth and was able to
look beyond his painful past and trust that God had
a future full of HOPE for him. He believed God was
orchestrating the circumstances of his life to bring about
a positive conclusion. Remember, that's what HOPE is:
Having Only Positive Expectations.

Having Only Positive Expectations

If you're a part of a fractured family, there's a good chance somebody has hurt you. You may bear the wounds of divorce, abandonment or abuse. Even though Joseph grew up in a messed up family, he didn't blame his upbringing on his problems. He endured being falsely accused of adultery and served jail time for a crime he never committed.

And then he did the most incredible thing of all. He forgave his brothers from his heart. The Bible tells us:

> His brothers then came and threw themselves down before him. "We are your slaves," they said. But Joseph said to them, "Don't be afraid. Am I in the place of God? You intended to harm me, but God intended it for good to accomplish what is now being done, the saving of many lives. So then, don't be afraid. I will provide for you and your children." And he reassured them and spoke kindly to them. (vv18-21)

This is what I like to call the Romans 8:28 of the Old Testament. Romans 8:28 reminds us that God is working all things—even your painful past—for the good of those who love Him and are called to do His will. God can give you the grace and strength to look at your past and say like Joseph, "You intended to harm me, *but God* intended it for good."

Having Only Positive Expectations

Those two words, "…but God" can make all the difference in your life.

19

G od can restore broken hearts and broken homes.
That doesn't necessarily mean God will just snap
His fingers and magically restore your family to what
it was like before that ugly incident or messy divorce.
Every choice has consequences. God lovingly forgives
sin and heals the brokenhearted, but He doesn't reverse
the consequences we set in motion by our poor choices.
**God just gives us the strength to move
forward and start a new page.**

If anybody deserved to nurse a grudge, it was Joseph.
It would have been easy for him to become bitter, but
he refused. Resentment is an acid that destroys its
container. God's Word says, "Get rid of all bitterness,
rage and anger, brawling and slander, along with every
form of malice." (Ephesians 4:31) Maybe you've gone
through a messy divorce. Or perhaps you're harboring
anger and resentment toward some family member who
has hurt you. Your bitterness will only destroy you.

The word "forgive" literally means, "to release." Years
ago, I knew a man in another church who had held a

grudge against his brother for years because he believed he cheated him in a business deal. Whenever he merely talked about his brother, he became enraged. He really struggled to forgive him. He told me, "But I'll never be able to forget what he's done to me." I told him that forgiving wasn't forgetting. Forgiveness simply involved releasing his brother from any desire to hurt him. I showed him Ephesians 4:32: "Be kind to one another, tenderhearted, forgiving one another, even as God for Christ's sake has forgiven you."

He said, "Okay, I'll try."

A few days later, he told me, "I tried to forgive my brother. I called him up and told him I needed to talk to him, but he refused to take my call. So, I don't guess I can forgive him."

I said, "Why do you think you need to talk to him to forgive him?"

He said, "Well, I wanted to tell him that if he asked me to, I'd be willing to forgive him." I told my friend he didn't need his brother's confession or permission to forgive him. He only needed the command of God to do it.

Reconciliation is not the same as forgiveness. Forgiveness is always a prerequisite of reconciliation, but forgiveness can occur *without* being reconciled. Reconciliation requires both parties to be in agreement. But forgiveness can be a one-way street. I told him to say out loud, "Right now, I forgive my brother for the rotten things he did to me." It took awhile but finally he said it. That's the day healing began in his life.

You can do the same. You can forgive someone without getting his or her permission to forgive you. Release them. Let them go. You may be thinking, "But they don't *deserve* my forgiveness." Joseph forgave his brothers for the sake of his father, Jacob—not because they deserved it. God doesn't forgive us for *our* sake; He forgives us for the sake of His Son. The Bible says we must forgive those who have hurt us, even as God, for Christ's sake, has forgiven us.

Having Only Positive Expectations

Having Only Positive Expectations

Having   Only   Positive   Expectations

When I've Passed My Prime

20

Someone said that old age is when you've got it all together, you just can't remember where you put it. At age eighty-five, Caleb was still going strong. In the book of Joshua, we find out that forty-five years earlier, Moses had promised him a piece of the Promised Land (Canaan) as God's reward for his faithfulness.

Caleb was one of the spies Moses sent out to investigate Canaan to see what kind of enemy the Israelites were up against. Although the majority of the 12 spies were afraid, he boldly reported back that God would make them victorious over the "giants" living in the land. Unfortunately, the Israelites wimped out and spent the next few decades wandering in the wilderness instead. Poor Caleb was stuck with a bunch of dissatisfied, unfaithful, whining people until Joshua, Moses' successor, led the people to victory. Even after 45 years, he still held onto God's promise and reminded Joshua that he had that property coming to him!

> "So on that day Moses swore to me, 'The land on which your feet have walked will be your

Having Only Positive Expectations

inheritance and that of your children forever, because you have followed the Lord my God wholeheartedly.' Now then, just as the Lord promised, he has kept me alive for forty-five years since the time he said this to Moses, while Israel moved about in the desert.

"So here I am today, eighty-five years old! I am still as strong today as the day Moses sent me out; I'm just as vigorous to go out to battle now as I was then. Now give me this hill country that the Lord promised me that day."
(Joshua 14:10-12)

One of the qualities I admire most about Caleb is his persistence. Has God given you a promise? Sure! In fact, He has given you hundreds and thousands of promises in His Word. According to *All the Promises in the Bible* by Herbert Lockyer, there are 7,457 of God's promises, and they are all yours to claim.

However, until you take hold of them by applying them to your life by faith, they don't do you any good. An unclaimed promise of God is like not claiming a winning lottery ticket. What if someone held a winning lottery ticket, but they never cashed it in to claim the prize? (Actually, they might be doing themselves a favor because studies show 80% of lottery winners end up declaring bankruptcy within five years!) What's worse than not claiming a winning lottery ticket is having the precious promises of God and not taking hold of them. In order to claim God's promises, you have to read them *and claim them.* **Once you claim one of God's promises, never release it.** Even if you have to wait a lifetime for it to be fulfilled!

One of my favorite stories is about a scrawny high kid from West Texas who attended a small high school. They didn't have a wrestling program, but he read a book on wrestling and asked one of the assistant football coaches if he would enter him in some of the wrestling matches in that region.

This little guy was neither strong, nor skillful, but he had one enduring quality—he refused to give up. His coach signed him up and to everyone's surprise he won every single wrestling match. By the end of the season, he was undefeated and even made it to the state finals. His opponent was a two-time state champ and a bona fide college prospect. Right away, the state champion made a couple of quick moves and soon had the West Texas kid pinned. The coach couldn't bear to watch his guy lose, so he turned his head away. Suddenly, the coach heard the roar of the crowd. He turned around and saw his kid was now on top of the state champ, pinning him down to win the match! The little guy bounced across the mat, hugged the coach and said, "Coach, I won! I won!"

The coach said, "What happened?"

He replied, "Coach, that guy was good. He had me twisted like a pretzel on that mat. But you know me, Coach. I never quit! I opened my eyes and there in front of my face was a big toe. I don't even know if it's against the rules or not, but I bit into that big toe with all my strength."

The coach cringed and the boy just smiled and said, "Coach, it's amazing what you can do when you bite your own toe!"

Caleb did whatever it took and he never gave up! He was eighty-five years old before he arrived at God's promise. That's an age when most people want to take time to slow down and step aside from their responsibilities. Not Caleb. God not only preserved the promise for the man—God preserved the *man* for the promise. God reminded Joshua and Caleb that He wasn't through with them yet. Joshua 13:1 says, "When Joshua was old and well advanced in years, the Lord said to him, 'You are very old, and there are still very large areas of land to be taken over.'" You'd expect God to say, "You've done a good job. Take a rest, boys, and I'll use some of these younger guys now." Nope. God needed a couple of octogenarians to seal the deal.

I'm not against retiring. Retiring from a *career* is a good idea—you've earned it, now go out and spend your children's inheritance! However, when you follow God wholeheartedly, you'll never retire from serving Him.

Having Only Positive Expectations

Six times in the Old Testament we read about Caleb: "... He wholeheartedly followed the Lord." In fact, Caleb's name literally means "follows God like a dog." If you aren't following God with your *whole* heart, you're only a half-hearted Christian.

Serving the Lord is not a job; it's a life calling. The word "vocation" comes from the Latin word "*vocare*" which means, "to call." God has called all of His children to serve Him. It's your real vocation—and you can't take a vacation from your vocation. You may think God can't use you because you're too old, or you don't have any special training or abilities. You may have given up HOPE, thinking your best days are behind you. One of the greatest servants of God in the 19th Century was a shoe salesman from Chicago named D.L. Moody. He was never ordained and he never attended college or seminary. But one time, D.L. Moody heard a preacher, Henry Varley, speak these words: "The world has yet to see what God can do in and with and through and for a man wholly committed to Him." And at that moment, D.L. Moody said, "By the grace of God I will be that man."

D.L. Moody shook two continents for Christ, including England. He was so uneducated that he once said to a group of very educated and sophisticated Englishmen, "Don't never think that God don't love you, for He do." As bad as his grammar was, God used him to bring thousands of British and American citizens to Christ.

Having Only Positive Expectations

He had the one ability God always honors: avail-ability.

When I was in my thirties, I thought I might retire from preaching when I was in my fifties. Now that I'm approaching sixty, I realize I will never retire from serving God. As long as I have teeth, I'm going to chew on the old devil, and even when I lose my teeth, I'm going to gum Him to distraction!

21

I once heard an amazing story of tenacity about a boy in Rochester, New York. An autistic student named Jason worked as the manager of the high school basketball team. Ja-Mac, as he's called, had never put on a uniform, but for the last game of the season his coach let him dress out. Toward the end of the game, he put Ja-Mac in to play. His first shot was an air ball that missed the goal by six feet. But pretty soon, he got hot. In the last four minutes of the game, Ja-Mac scored 20 points, including six three-point bombs. After the game, the students and team lifted Ja-Mac onto their shoulders and celebrated! Stories like Jason's remind us that victory comes in "cans"—defeat comes in "can'ts."

When the Israelite spies saw the giants residing in the land of Canaan, some of them said they felt like "grasshoppers in our own eyes" compared to the mighty warriors of Canaan (Numbers 13:33) Ten of the spies suffered from what I call a "grasshopper complex." They were already defeated in their minds because they'd given up HOPE.

Having Only Positive Expectations

However, they were only *half* right. They *did* look like grasshoppers in their *own* eyes. But to the Canaanites, they appeared to be a mighty army. In fact, the people in Canaan had been trembling in fear of the Israelite army for 40 years! You may be suffering from a grasshopper complex, thinking you are too little or too insignificant to matter. If you hear "you can't do it" enough, you may begin to believe it.

Caleb didn't deny there were giants. Instead, he said in Numbers 14:9 that those giants would be "bread for us." In God's power, they would have them for lunch! The wimpy spies were whining, "Look how big those giants are compared to us!" Caleb said, "Look how small those giants are compared to God!" The worrywarts whined, "They're too big for us to fight." Caleb said, "They're too big for us to miss!"

Just because you're facing some giant-sized problems doesn't mean it's hopeless. Seemingly hopeless situations call for courage. In his book, *One Crowded Hour*, Tim Burton wrote about some Nepalese soldiers in Borneo in 1964. The Gurkhas, as they were called, were known for their valor. A British commander once asked a squad of Gurkhas if they would be willing to jump out of an airplane into combat against the enemy. After discussing it for a moment, the Gurkha sergeant replied, "Yes, we will jump out, if the airplane will fly as slow as possible only 100 feet above a swamp." The British commander said, "But that's too low. Your parachutes wouldn't have time to open." The Gurkha sergeant said, "Oh, you didn't mention parachutes." Now, that's courage! They were willing to jump out of an airplane without parachutes!

Ephesians 6:10-11 says, "Be strong in the Lord and in his mighty power. Put on the full armor of God so that you can take your stand against the devil's schemes." In your own strength, you are as helpless as a newborn kitten. But when you depend on God's strength, you have all the power of the Lion of the Tribe of Judah! You may face an uncertain future and it may seem all HOPE is lost, but just remember, the word "impossible" is not part of God's vocabulary. It may be impossible in your strength, but you must claim this promise: "I can do everything through him who gives me strength." (Philippians 4:13)

Having Only Positive Expectations

Having Only Positive Expectations

HOPE

Having   Only   Positive   Expectations

When I'm Worried about the Future

22

President Franklin Roosevelt once addressed the nation with these chilling words: "Yesterday, December 7, 1941—a date which will live in infamy—the United States of America was suddenly and deliberately attacked by naval and air forces of the Empire of Japan." He concluded his speech with these words of HOPE: "With confidence in our armed forces—with the unbounded determination of our people—we will gain the inevitable triumph—so help us God." After four years of bloody combat in which 300,000 American soldiers died, there was dancing in the streets after Germany and Japan surrendered in 1945. The end of WWII brought a sense of closure to the attack on Pearl Harbor.

But America's enemies would strike again.

On September 11, 2001, most Americans remember where they were when they first heard that jets had crashed into the World Trade Center and the Pentagon. That evening, President Bush spoke these words to America: "Today, our fellow citizens, our way of life, our very freedom came under attack in a series of deliberate and deadly terrorist acts. The pictures of airplanes flying into buildings, fires burning, huge structures collapsing, have filled us with disbelief, terrible sadness and a quiet, unyielding anger. These acts of mass murder were intended to frighten our nation into chaos and retreat. But they have failed. Our country is strong."

He concluded his remarks: "Tonight, I ask for your prayers for all those who grieve, for the children whose worlds have been shattered, for all whose sense of safety and security has been threatened. And I pray they will be comforted by a power greater than any of us, spoken through the ages in Psalm 23: 'Even though I walk through the valley of the shadow of death, I fear no evil, for You are with me.'"

More than a decade later, we aren't dancing in the streets, because this war against Islamic extremists is still raging. This is not a war that will end with the signing of a peace treaty between two governments. It may be a long time before we find any sense of closure from the events of 9/11. In spite of the ongoing war against terrorism, God has still been faithful to us. As we look to the future, we should not be filled with fear. Instead, we can face each day Having Only Positive Expectations!

One of God's greatest promises is found in Proverbs 23:17-18, "Do not let your heart envy sinners, but always be zealous for the fear of the Lord. There is surely a future hope for you, and your hope will not be cut off." The existentialist says there is no tomorrow, there is only today. A teenager says tomorrow can't get here fast enough. A senior citizen says tomorrow is already here. **But a child of God can say tomorrow is full of HOPE.**

The Bible says, "Do not boast about tomorrow, for you do not know what a day may bring forth." (Proverbs 27:1) Throughout the ages, people have tried to predict the future, but their best predictions have largely been proven wrong. Consider these predictions that went amiss:

> "Theoretically, television may be feasible, but I consider it an impossibility—a development we should waste little time dreaming about." (Lee de Forest, 1926, inventor of the cathode ray tube)

> "I think there is a world market for about five computers." (Thomas J. Watson, 1943, Chairman of the Board of IBM)

> "We don't think the Beatles will do anything in their market. Guitar groups are on their way out." (Recording company expert, 1962)

God says about people who boast about knowing the future, "Now listen, you who say, 'Today or tomorrow we will go to this or that city, spend a year there, carry

Having Only Positive Expectations

on business and make money.' Why, you do not even know what will happen tomorrow. What is your life? You are a mist that appears for a little while and then vanishes. Instead, you ought to say, 'If it is the Lord's will, we will live and do this or that.' As it is, you boast and brag. All such boasting is evil." (James 4:13-16)

You can't know the future, but there is one thing you *can* know: compared to eternity, the span of our lives is like a mist. The Bible doesn't prohibit you from making plans—it teaches the importance of wise planning. **Just don't leave God out of those plans.** As you make your plans you must say, "If the Lord wills..." Only by seeking God's will can you face the future with HOPE. Life is so short—it's just a mist. Let's live everyday as if it were our last!

23

Father Mychal Judge served as a chaplain for the New York Fire Department for ten years. When the fire station alarm sounded on 9/11, Chaplain Judge was nearby. He threw on a fireproof suit and ran immediately toward the burning buildings. He was struck and killed by falling debris and became the first known casualty outside of the buildings. You have likely seen a picture of five firemen carrying his body out of the rubble. They found a hand-written prayer in Father Judge's pocket, which has since been named Mychal's prayer: "Lord, take me where You want me to go; Let me meet who You want me to meet; Tell me what You want me to say, and keep me out of Your way." That's the attitude of a man who is trusting God for the future!

You might not boast about what you'll do in the future—your problem may be just the opposite. Maybe you're so worried about the future that you're afraid to make any plans at all. Our English word "worry" comes from the German word *würgen*, which means, "to strangle." Jesus said about worry: "Look at the birds of the air; they do not sow or reap or store away in barns, and yet your heavenly Father feeds them. Are you not much more valuable than they? Who of you by worrying can add a single hour to his life? ...But seek first his kingdom and his righteousness, and all these things will be given to you as well. Therefore do not worry about tomorrow, for tomorrow will worry about itself. Each day has enough trouble of its own." (Matthew 6:26-27; 33-34)

If you have a problem with fear and worry, you need to become a "birdwatcher." They don't worry—God takes care of them. If you don't believe it, ask a veterinarian if they've ever treated a wild bird for anxiety disorder and see what they say. I once read a poem about an imaginary conversation between a robin and a sparrow:

> Said the robin to the sparrow; I'd really like to know;
> Why these anxious human creatures rush about and worry so?
> Said the sparrow to the robin, I suppose that it must be;
> That they have no Heavenly Father such as cares for you and me.
> (author unknown)

The great British Baptist pastor Charles Spurgeon once said, "God is too good to be unkind, He is too wise to be mistaken, and when you cannot trace His hand, you can always trust His heart." Worry is not just

a weakness—it is a sin! You may not realize
that worry calls God a liar. God has promised us that
He will never leave or forsake us. However, when we
worry, we're saying, "I don't believe you, God." God has
promised He will supply all your needs according to
His riches in Christ Jesus. When you worry about your
needs, you're saying, "I just can't believe God." God has
said over and over in His Word, "Do not worry. Do not
fear. Do not let your heart be troubled." Whenever we
worry, we are essentially declaring, "Maybe God doesn't
know what He's talking about!" Worry and faith are
mutually exclusive.

When the Bible says you shouldn't worry about the
future, it doesn't mean you should just put your mind in
neutral and glibly say, "Whatever." No! There are things
we can do instead of worrying, starting with prayer.

If you can *do* something about a troubling situation,
don't *worry*. *Do* what you can to resolve it. But if there's
nothing you can do about a situation (like the weather,
for example) don't worry about it—worrying only
makes a problem worse. One of my favorite poems
reads:

> For every evil under the sun
> Either there is a cure or there is none.
> If there be one seek 'till you find it.
> If there be none, never mind it!
> (author unknown)

Having Only Positive Expectations

Worry is stewing without doing! Don't worry about
tomorrow; trust God's heart—even if you can't see His
hand.

Having Only Positive Expectations

HOPE

Having   Only   Positive   Expectations

When I'm Grieving

24

In 2005, I preached a message from Job called, "What to Do When Your World Crumbles." Several people commented to me afterwards that they thought my message title was in response to the terrible devastation caused by Hurricane Katrina that had occurred just five days prior. However, I always plan my message titles a year or more in advance. There is no way I could have known that Sunday would mark a time of unprecedented pain and suffering in our nation. But God knew.

Job was a righteous guy who was blessed with great wealth and a wonderful family. At a gathering in heaven, Satan told God that the only reason Job served God was because he was so blessed. He charged that if Job lost it all, he would curse God to His face. God knew Job's heart, but in order to demonstrate it for Satan and all the hosts of angels, both good and bad, God gave Satan permission to test his theory. Satan went to work and Job suffered the loss of his livelihood and his family in one day—just like what happened to so many of Katrina's victims.

Life has a way of crumbling in without warning.

When he heard the news, Job tore his robe and shaved his head. (Job 1:20) His reaction is a little confusing to us today. The tearing of clothes was a customary way of expressing immediate grief in the ancient world. You've probably felt so much inner pain before that you wanted to tear something. Tearing cloth is a metaphor for a broken heart. There's the strain of pulling and the release when the cloth tears. Tearing his clothes was an immediate expression of his grief, but shaving his head was a long-term expression of his pain. Every time he felt the chill on his scalp, he would be reminded of his heartache. As his hair grew out, it was also a gradual reminder to him that life goes on. Often, with time, the pain lessens.

When you're hurting, it's okay to express your grief. Moreover, it's *important* to express your feelings. Submerging your tears behind a brave face can lead to unhealthy emotional problems. To express your grief, you need to understand what grief is. Change + Loss = Grief

Change is never easy. Job lost the equivalent of tens of millions of dollars in the span of a few minutes when raiders carried off all his livestock and murdered his workers. It would be as if you lost your job, your bank account, your investments and your retirement account in one day. On the heels of hearing of the loss of his wealth, Job learned his children were dead. His three daughters and seven sons were gathered in a house when a killer storm blew in. The walls of the building collapsed and they all died.

Job didn't deny his grief. He didn't slap a fake smile on his face and flippantly say, "Everything is going to be okay." He cried long and hard. In chapter 16, Job admitted how deeply he was grieving. He said, "I have sewed sackcloth over my skin and buried my brow in the dust. My face is red with weeping, deep shadows ring my eyes." (Job 16:15-16)

The greater the sense of loss, the greater the depth of your grief. I've been told there is nothing to compare with the depth of grief from losing a child. But death isn't the only thing that causes grief. When you lose a job, you grieve. When you lose a mate through divorce or death, you grieve. When you lose a friend, you grieve. You may even lose a house to fire or flood and grieve. Whatever the nature of your loss, it's important to express your grief honestly. It doesn't show a lack of faith to cry a river of tears.

Even in the midst of our pain over what we have lost, we still have HOPE. Jesus was a Man of Sorrows acquainted with grief. He wept out of compassion for Mary and Martha at their brother's grave, even though He planned to resuscitate Lazarus. On another occasion, Jesus was so heartbroken over the sinful people in Jerusalem that He stood atop a hill overlooking the city and wept bitter tears. It's okay to grieve. In fact, it's good.

After he cried, Job collapsed. But he didn't collapse into hopelessness. He fell down to worship God. When you're hurting, that's probably the last thing that is on your mind. But we need to understand why this is a key step in the grieving process.

25

I've performed over 1,000 funerals over the years, and I've yet to see a U-Haul following the hearse in a funeral procession. It's true—you can't take it with you.

Job said when he collapsed in worship before God, "Naked I came from my mother's womb, and naked I will depart. The Lord gave and the Lord has taken away; may the name of the Lord be praised." (Job 1:21)

Some people think everything good in their life has come to them because they earned it. Others think society owes them a living or that they deserve to have all their needs met. However, the Bible says that everything good in life is a *gift* from God above. "Every good and perfect gift is from above, coming down from the Father of the heavenly lights, who does not change like shifting shadows." (James 1:17)

If the Lord gave us everything we have, we must also accept that He may take something away without giving us a reason. Still, that didn't stop Job from trying to find out why all this misfortune happened to him. Job asks the Lord some tough questions. He asks, "Why me?" in a variety of ways, but he never receives an answer. God never gives Job a reason for why these things happened. As far as we know, God never even let Job in on the deal with the devil. Instead, God spends four chapters at the end of Job reminding him that His wisdom, greatness and power are far beyond our ability to comprehend. If you think you deserve an answer to the question, "Why did this happen?" then your concept of God is too small. There will always be a sense of mystery and awe about Him.

In the book of Romans, Paul is writing about God's plan for the ages and he suddenly exclaims, "Oh, the depth of the riches of the wisdom and knowledge of God! How unsearchable are his judgments, and his paths beyond tracing out! Who has known the mind of the Lord? Or been his counselor? Who has ever given to God that God should repay him?" (Romans 11:33-35)

When you've lost something or someone precious, it is easy to forget that "the Lord gives… and the Lord takes away." He doesn't owe us a reason. John Claypool was a pastor in Louisville, Kentucky when I was in seminary. He and his wife lost their daughter, Laura Lou, to leukemia. He told me about what happened by telling a story from his childhood. During WWII, his family didn't own a washing machine. Gas was rationed and they couldn't afford to drive to a laundry. Keeping their clothes clean became a daily challenge. John's neighbor

Having Only Positive Expectations

went to war and his wife moved in with her family. They offered to let John's family use their Bendix washer while they were gone. It became John's chore to help with the family's laundry, and he actually developed a fondness for that old green Bendix. When the war eventually ended, his neighbors returned and they reclaimed their washing machine.

Over the course of the war, young John had actually forgotten the machine was loaned to them. When the neighbors removed it, John was upset and angry that they would take "his" washing machine. His mother sat him down and said, "John, you must remember that the washing machine never belonged to us in the first place. That we ever got to use it at all was a gift. So, instead of being mad at it being taken away, let's use this as an occasion to be thankful."

As John struggled with the death of his daughter years later, he remembered that old green Bendix. He wrote, "When I remember that Laura Lou was a gift, pure and simple, something I neither earned nor deserved nor had a right to; and when I remember that the appropriate response to a gift, even when it is taken away, is gratitude, then I am better able to try and thank God that I was ever given her in the first place" (*Steps of a Fellow Struggler*). That's exactly how Job felt. He knew every good thing in his life had come from God, and God had the right to take anything away.

Having Only Positive Expectations

26

Have you ever heard the advice, "Cheer up, things could be worse?" Job cheered up, and sure enough things got worse! Satan attacked Job's health and made him deathly ill.

What do you think Job *felt* like doing when that happened? There was a Mrs. Job in this story and she told her husband to do what most anyone would feel like doing. In Job 2:9, she told Job to "curse God and die." That's what she felt like doing, and Job probably shared her feelings. But Job didn't live by feelings; he lived by faith. When you are hurting, you have to make the choice, by faith, to praise God.

It's easy to offer praise to God when everything is wonderful in your life. But when you offer God praise in the midst of your pain, it becomes a precious sacrifice. The Bible says, "Through Jesus, therefore, let us continually offer to God a sacrifice of praise—the fruit of lips that confess his name." (Hebrews 13:15)

There is one thing *not* to do when your world crumbles

in: blame God. Notice the last words in chapter 1: "In all this, Job did not sin by charging God with wrongdoing." Whenever we suffer, we immediately look for someone to blame. If we can blame our suffering on our parents, our spouse, our co-workers or society in general, we can justify our bitterness. That prevents us from moving on to becoming whole again. God gets blamed for a lot of suffering today. But in spite of his pain, and his unanswered questions, Job never charged that God was wrong.

One morning when I was getting ready to shave, I read the label on the side of the can of shaving cream. It said, "Caution, contents under pressure. Do not incinerate or puncture." If you burn or puncture a can of shaving cream, the high pressure will cause the can to explode. That describes what a lot of people are going through these days. They are living under intense pressure and stress, and they may be only a few degrees away from an explosion. They can't stand the heat and they don't know how to get out of the kitchen.

If you want to know a person's character, observe what happens when he or she is under great stress. Jeremiah 17:9 says, "The heart is deceitful above all things, and desperately wicked, who can know it?" Whatever is on the inside will come out under pressure. If your sense of worth and happiness is defined by your possessions, then prepare to be devastated. But if your joy is based upon a living relationship with a loving God, nothing can separate you from His love.

Having Only Positive Expectations

Whenever you're going through a tough time, there's always the fear of the unknown. Job must have been afraid of what his life would be like without his family, but he put his trust firmly in God.

Before 1492 when Columbus sailed the ocean blue, the common belief was that if a ship from Europe sailed too far west, they would either fall off the edge of the world or face terrible danger. In England, the story is told about an ancient nautical map dating back to the time of King Henry IV. On it, the mapmakers had written these words over the Atlantic Ocean: "Here be dragons; Here be demons; Here be danger." Based on those superstitious warnings, sailors were afraid of sailing there. However, an English navigator named John Franklin was a mighty man of God. He took that same map and crossed out those fearful words and added: "Here Be God!"

As you sail toward your darkest fears and deepest worries, *here be God*! He is there to keep you and sustain you. Job said, "I *know* that my Redeemer lives…" (Job 19:25)

Having Only Positive Expectations

Having   Only   Positive   Expectations

When Life's Storms Roll

27

On October 26, 1991, the Andrea Gail, a 72-foot fishing boat, was in the North Atlantic. The six-man crew had been fishing for swordfish and the ship was attempting to return to its port in Gloucester, Massachusetts. Suddenly, a rare combination of weather systems came together to form what was later dubbed "the perfect storm" by the author Sebastian Junger. A weather satellite image taken on October 30 shows the remnants of Hurricane Grace swirling together with a polar air mass charging down from Canada. The result was an explosive storm with recorded winds in excess of 150 mph and the largest waves ever measured. The waves crested at the height of a ten-story building with a pressure of six tons per square foot of water.

The Andrea Gail never stood a chance against that monster storm. The last recorded radio transmission from the captain was, "She's comin' on boys, and she's comin' on strong!" I can only imagine the feeling of dread they felt as they heard the howling wind and watched the huge waves building.

You may be struggling right now because difficult circumstances and unfavorable situations have come together in your life to create a perfect storm of trouble. In Matthew, we read about how the disciples found themselves in a raging storm. The Sea of Galilee is actually a beautiful freshwater lake six miles wide and fourteen miles long. At 600 feet below sea level, it's the lowest lake on the planet. It's surrounded by tall mountains, which can act like a funnel. A storm can roll in with amazing ferocity. Mark tells us the disciples' journey was at night. With no stars by which to steer, it had to have been a frightening experience.

"Then he got into the boat and his disciples followed him. Without warning, a furious storm came up on the lake, so that the waves swept over the boat. But Jesus was sleeping. The disciples went and woke him, saying, 'Lord, save us! We're going to drown!' He replied, 'You of little faith, why are you so afraid?' Then he got up and rebuked the winds and the waves, and it was completely calm. The men were amazed and asked, 'What kind of man is this? Even the winds and the waves obey him!'" (Matthew 8:23-28)

Have you ever been outside when suddenly the air grew still and quiet? It's almost as if the birds stop singing and fly for cover. Even though there isn't a drop of water falling, you can see the sky getting dark and even smell the rain on the horizon. That phenomenon is the basis for the old saying, "It's just the calm before the storm."

Having Only Positive Expectations

There is actually some scientific truth to that saying. Meteorologists report that as a cumulonimbus cell starts building, strong updrafts inside the cell create a vacuum effect and the air becomes heavy and quiet before the storm erupts.

On those rare occasions when life seems to be calm and peaceful, some people say it's "just the calm before the storm." They *expect* their situation to get worse and guess what? It usually does! When we place our HOPE in Christ, it's much different. We know that when bad things happen it's "just the *storm* before the *calm!*" In other words, we can count on Jesus stilling the waves and calming the sea—like He did for the disciples in this story.

Some Christians make the mistake of thinking that just because they have the Lord in their life they will be exempt from trouble. Even though Jesus was in the boat with the disciples, the storm still struck. And even if Jesus is in your life, you will still encounter storms. There are physical storms, financial storms, emotional storms and relational storms—all of which can strike suddenly with no warning. It doesn't mean that God doesn't love you or that He is punishing you. Jesus *led* the disciples into this storm to teach them to trust Him.

The Bible says, "Dear friends, do not be surprised at the painful trial you are suffering, as though something strange were happening to you." (1 Peter 4:12) The Bible isn't a feel-good book about people who lived perfect lives. It traces the lives of hundreds of people who struggled with pain and suffering, yet maintained their faith in God.

28

When Franklin Delano Roosevelt delivered his first of four inaugural addresses in 1933, the nation was in the grip of the Great Depression. Times were tough. Trying to reassure a nation on the verge of panic, he said, "This is preeminently the time to speak the truth, the whole truth, frankly and boldly... So first of all let me assert my firm belief that the only thing we have to fear is fear itself—nameless, unreasoning, unjustified terror..."

The phrase, "We have nothing to fear but fear itself" became a famous saying. The reason why some banks failed is because customers *feared* they would fail, so they withdrew their money. As the rumor spread, thousands more people rushed to the banks, which caused the banks to close.

The late Paul Harvey loved to tell the story of the Arkansas farmer who kept losing hens to a nocturnal predator. He suspected it was a fox. So, one night he left his loaded shotgun beside his bed. When he heard a commotion in the henhouse, he jumped out of bed

wearing only his nightshirt and grabbed his shotgun.
As he approached the dark henhouse, he began to
worry, "What if this fox is rabid and it bites me before
I can kill it? Or what if it's not a fox, but a wildcat?" He
was literally shaking with fear as he approached. As he
paused to listen, his trusty hound dog, Blue, crept up
silently behind his master. The dog affectionately stuck
his nose under the nightshirt and "cold nosed" the
farmer. "Kablam!" Thirty hens lost their lives that night.
Paul Harvey used to say, "It wasn't the shotgun that
killed them... it was fear."

When the disciples cried out to Jesus to do something
about the storm, He said, "You of little faith, why are you
so afraid?" The disciples were fighting two storms that
night. The first was the physical storm around them; the
other was the invisible fear raging in their minds. **Fear
can cause more damage than whatever it is
you fear!**

God says, "So do not fear, for I am with you; do not be
dismayed, for I am your God. I will strengthen you and
help you; I will uphold you with my righteous right
hand." (Isaiah 41:10) What causes you to be afraid?
Would your feelings change if you could actually *see* God
with you? If you could *feel* Him holding you up with His
right hand? He tells you not to be afraid because He *is*
there!

While the storm was raging, do you know what Jesus

was doing? He was sleeping! The waves were crashing
and the winds were howling. The disciples were stressed
out and Jesus was snoring away. Two words have never
been heard in heaven: "Uh oh!" Corrie ten Boom once
said, "There is no panic in heaven—only plans."

I once had a friend who operated an air charter service
flying a Beechcraft King Air. Since I was also a pilot,
there were several occasions when Jeff called me to serve
as his co-pilot.

Early one Sunday morning, we flew to Montgomery,
Alabama to pick up a former all-pro linebacker for the
Miami Dolphins to speak at our church. He was part
of the 1972 undefeated Dolphins squad and he was
tough as nails. As we boarded the King Air to return
to Montgomery that afternoon, thunderstorms were
building along our flight route. We climbed to altitude
and it was a very bumpy ride. The King Air had weather
radar so we could see where the heaviest cells were. Jeff
flew a heading that took us between the heaviest cells,
but it was still a rough flight. Our passenger was a brave
football player, but he was a very nervous flyer. He kept
saying, "Why don't we just land? I'm getting sick back
here!"

As we approached Dannelly Field in Montgomery, Jeff
and I could see on the radar that there was a strong cell
near the airport, but the weather at the airport itself was
clear. The line of thunderstorms was still to the west.

We were in dark clouds with rain and thunder around us and the visibility was almost zero. The football player kept yelling from the back, "I can't take much more of this!" I looked at the radar and could tell we were almost out of the storm, so I turned around and said, "Hang on just a minute longer and we'll be out of the storm, I promise!" I could tell he didn't believe me because he was sweating profusely and was a little green around the gills. In about 60 seconds, we broke out of the storm where the air was smooth and the visibility was unlimited. We were perfectly lined up with the runway and made a smooth landing. While our passenger was sick with worry, neither Jeff nor I were concerned. We could see the radar and we trusted the ability of the King Air to fly through turbulence and rain.

Jesus said, "I have told you these things, so that *in me*, you may have peace. In this world you will have trouble. But take heart! I have overcome the world." (John 16:33) Jesus didn't say, "…*with me* you'll have peace." We are "in Christ" the same way that Noah was "in" the ark. Noah, his family and the animals were safe in the ark when the ark was in the storm. That's what it means for us to be "in Christ." Jesus can sleep through a storm, and if you are in Christ, you can find rest in the midst of your storms as well.

Having Only Positive Expectations

29

Several of Jesus' disciples were seasoned fishermen. They had grown up on these waters. They probably did everything they could to survive the storm. They trimmed the sail, turned the boat into the wind and started bailing. But finally they came to what I call the POTD: The Point of Total Desperation. They gave up and cried out, "Lord, save us! We're going to drown." I love the simplicity of that prayer. They didn't use a lot of flowery words like, "Dear Lord, as we come to you on this stormy evening, wouldst thou consider our plight?"

No, they just said, "Save us!"

The Bible says, "Everyone that calls on the name of the Lord will be saved." (Romans 10:13) Some people think that only applies to our initial salvation experience. But that's a promise we should claim daily. Every time we find ourselves in a storm of suffering, we should call on the Lord to deliver us. The Bible says, "The righteous cry out, and the Lord hears them; he delivers them from all their troubles. The Lord is close to the brokenhearted and saves those who are crushed in spirit." (Psalm

34:17-18) Is your heart broken? Is your spirit crushed?
**Call upon the Lord and He will deliver
you from your troubles.**

I can imagine Jesus making His way to the front of the
boat, the fierce wind whipping His hair and beard. The
lightning is flashing and the thunder is crashing. Water
from the pounding waves soaks through His robe. The
Bible says, "Then he got up and rebuked the winds and
the waves, and it was completely calm." (Matthew 8:26)

In Mark's account of this same story, Jesus used a word
that a parent would use to reassure a troubled child. A
good translation is, "Hush, now. Just calm down." At
that, the storm vanished instantly. Then I imagine Jesus
resumed His nap!

Of course, every storm eventually ends. Gradually. The
point of this miracle was the *suddenness* of the calm.
There was instantaneous tranquility. In a flash, the wind
and the rain were gone and the water was as smooth
as glass. The only sound was the ragged breath of the
disciples and the pounding of their hearts. I'm sure
there was another sound too: the sound of twelve jaws
dropping and hitting the deck. The Bible says they were
amazed at what happened.

In over 40 years of ministry, I've seen hundreds of
Christians go through times of unimaginable pain
and stress. Yet many of them possess a sense of peace

Having Only Positive Expectations

and calm that is beyond human understanding. That's exactly the kind of peace the Bible promises. "And the peace of God, which transcends all understanding, will guard your hearts and your minds in Christ Jesus." (Philippians 4:7) It's like the Secret Service agents who surround the President. Their job is to protect and guard him from all harm. In exactly the same way, God's peace can surround your mind and guard your thought life. The Secret Service agents are trained to prevent anything that threatens the life of the President. God's peace can protect your mind from fearful thoughts that threaten to harm you.

Why were the disciples out on the boat in the first place? Where were they going? Mark tells us that Jesus said when they first stepped in the boat, "Let us go over to the other side..." (Mark 4:35) In the midst of the storm, the disciples forgot the original plan. Once Jesus said they were going "to the other side," all the armies of Caesar could not have sunk their boat. Jesus has promised His followers that we'll make it safely through every storm to the other side. Philippians 1:6 says, "He who began a good work in you will carry it on to completion." If the disciples had just trusted His Word, they wouldn't have been afraid of drowning.

If Jesus is in your boat, you're going to make it to the other side!

When I was a pastor in my late twenties, Don and Pat

were good friends who were going through a storm with their teenage daughter. Don was an easy-going person, but Pat worried about anything and everything. I had just recently preached on this miracle, and Pat sent me a note that said, "The only thing I remember from your sermon was 'Jesus is in my boat so I know I'll get to the other side.' I'm hanging on to that promise." That storm passed, but within a year, Don discovered he had Hodgkin's disease. As he was dying, Pat wrote me a letter. At the bottom she wrote, "Jesus is in my boat, so I know I'll get to the other side." After a long battle, Don died at the age of forty-three. I could hardly speak during his funeral because we were so close.

When I accepted the call to pastor another church, Pat wrote me again telling me she was still struggling with her pain and grief. After she signed her name, she wrote: "…but Jesus is in my boat and I know I'll get to the other side." We stayed in touch through the years, and Pat remarried. Life is good and she loves being a grandmother. A few years ago, I was in Alabama and Pat invited me to dinner. For dessert she brought in a cake decorated with a boat and a figure of Jesus standing in the boat. Can you guess what the words on the cake said? "Jesus is still in my boat, and I know I'll get to the other side!"

Having   Only   Positive   Expectations

When America Needs It Most

30

America has seen amazing technological advancements during the past 50 years, but during the same period we have witnessed alarming moral decline. America was founded as a haven for people seeking liberty to practice their faith without persecution. I wonder what George Washington's or Benjamin Franklin's reaction would be if they could ride a time machine from 1776 to today. What would they think of our depraved culture and our huge federal bureaucracy? We know where America has been, but where do you think we are heading? Is there HOPE for America?

In a word, yes. But not until and unless we experience true revival.

The church I grew up in had a "revival" every spring and fall. A guest preacher and guest musician came in to lead weeklong services and people seemed to enjoy them. But most of these events were simply "meetings" and not true revivals. The English word for "revival" comes from two Latin phrases, *re*, which means "again" and *vivere*, which means, "to live." Revival basically means to "live again." If a person suffers a heart attack, CPR can often be used to "revive" that person. Revival is restoring spiritual vitality to a lifeless body... whether that is a family, church or even an entire nation."

A spiritually lifeless person is someone who has lost his or her zeal. Their spiritual life is dull, dead and despondent. Have you ever been more excited about Jesus or more faithful to Jesus than you are at this moment? If you answer "yes," you need to experience revival.

Whenever pastors talk about America needing a spiritual revival, they often quote 2 Chronicles 7:14: "... if my people, who are called by my name, will humble themselves and pray and seek my face and turn from their wicked ways, then will I hear from heaven and will forgive their sin and will heal their land." But do you know the context for this verse?

Solomon had just completed a beautiful new Temple for the Lord, which took seven years to build. Over 160,000 workers were involved in the construction. The Temple contained several tons of pure gold worth hundreds of millions of dollars today. They had a weeklong dedication celebration when it opened. Things were going great—the people had never been happier and their offerings were huge. But it is exactly at this point God spoke the words in 2 Chronicles 7.

When Solomon had finished the temple of the
LORD and the royal palace, and had succeeded
in carrying out all he had in mind to do in the
temple of the LORD and in his own palace, the
LORD appeared to him at night and said:
"I have heard your prayer and have chosen
this place for myself as a temple for sacrifices.
When I shut up the heavens so that there is no
rain, or command locusts to devour the land
or send a plague among my people, Now my
eyes will be open and my ears attentive to the
prayers offered in this place … But if you turn
away and forsake the decrees and commands
I have given you and go off and serve other
gods and worship them, then I will uproot
Israel from my land, which I have given them,
and will reject this temple I have consecrated
for my Name. I will make it a byword and an
object of ridicule among all peoples."
(2 Chronicles 7:11-20)

At the time, Israel was the leading world superpower.
Even Egypt's Queen of Sheba came to see the glory of
Israel. Within about 275 years of this warning, however,
the nation of Israel became corrupt and depraved and
fell to the Assyrians. A few years later, the Babylonians
destroyed the nation of Judah, along with Jerusalem and
the Temple.

America stands as the military world leader, but we also

Having Only Positive Expectations

lead the world in divorce, violence and pornography. The consequences of our national transgressions are catching up with us. I pray we will turn to God before it's too late.

31

Like a good fire marshal tracing a fire to determine its source, historians can generally trace where and when a spark of revival ignited because it affected the spiritual and moral climate of an entire region. After two or three generations of settlers established themselves in the New World, wickedness and depravity began to creep into cities like Boston. The human instrument of the first Great Awakening was Jonathan Edwards, a highly educated minister. He later became the third president of Princeton University. Edwards was a small man who wore spectacles with thick lenses. He read his sermons word for word in a thin, monotone voice. But the power of God was so strong through his preaching that the men and women listening cried out and literally grabbed onto the wooden support pillars inside the church to keep from "falling" into hell.

In a short period of time, over 30,000 residents of New England were converted and the revival fires spread throughout the Thirteen Colonies. This spiritual awakening fanned the flames of the colonists' efforts to secure independence from England. Many respected historians claim America's freedom-spirit was born during a revival. Both Edwards and John Wesley, who was a contemporary revival leader in England, were deeply influenced by a group of German Christians called Moravians. Ten years earlier in 1724, Count Nicolas Zinzendorf, a bishop of the Moravian Church, gathered a group of people to pray for the conversion of the lost in Europe. This prayer meeting actually continued 24 hours a day for 100 years! News of this prayer movement "across the pond" motivated Edwards to pray for the conversion of his congregation in the New World. He became burdened because many of the people attending his church were not Christians. Thousands of "churchgoers" were converted during the First Great Awakening. Records indicate at least one-third of the total population of the Colonies was converted to Christ through this sweeping revival.

The Second Great Awakening was in 1841 in New York and the Midwest. After the Revolutionary War and the War of 1812, thousands more new settlers came to the New World and many moved westward into the wilderness of Ohio and Kentucky. Once again, sin and wickedness ruled in many of the cities and in the pioneer regions. These were the days of the camp meetings. Families piled into wagons and buggies and traveled to a designated place to spend a couple of weeks in a time of fellowship, preaching and worship after the crops were "laid by" each August. Many of the families were so isolated that they packed an entire year of church into this short period of time!

Having Only Positive Expectations

One notable camp meeting I researched took place near Cane Ridge, Kentucky. At a time when the entire population of the region was around 50,000 people, over 25,000 people gathered in August for the Cane Ridge camp meeting. A group of Cumberland Presbyterians had designated every Saturday as a day of fasting and prayer for two years before this event, praying for God to do a great work. And He did—thousands came to know Christ as Savior and Lord.

As this second wave of revival spread throughout America, it touched a young lawyer who became one of its most effective preachers. Charles G. Finney was converted to Christ while reading the book of Romans as a requirement for a legal course. He traveled around the country preaching the Gospel and entire cities were converted. His eyes were so deep set and piercing, it was said that one look from him caused some people to fall on their knees in repentance. In every city, he preached against social injustice, including slavery and child labor. This great awakening ultimately gave birth to the later emancipation of slaves. In true revival, individuals are converted, Christians are restored to vitality, cities are changed and an entire culture is affected.

During the 20th century, there have been isolated outbreaks of revival. There was a great surge of evangelism after WWII during the 1950s. There was the Jesus Movement of the 1970s, and we saw promising signs in the 1990s, but nothing has affected our national moral position. In fact, we continue to slide backwards spiritually and morally.

I believe God wants to send a great spiritual awakening to our nation again—it's our only HOPE.

32

It can no longer be said that America is the moral conscience of our world. Our cries for global human rights sound empty and hypocritical to people in other countries because they know we lead the world in divorce, violence, abortion and crime. When I traveled to Europe for the first time, I was amazed to learn many Europeans are *afraid* to travel to America.

Fifty years ago, it wasn't just Bible-believing Christians who spoke out against adultery, divorce and homosexual behavior. Our society as a whole disapproved. Today, not only are these common practices in our society—many churches are marrying same-sex partners and ordaining openly gay individuals. If a Christian stands up and speaks out against sin, he or she is labeled an intolerant, narrow-minded bigot. I agree with Billy Graham who said in the 1970s, "If God doesn't judge America, He owes an apology to Sodom and Gomorrah!"

Alexis de Tocqueville, a famous French political philosopher, visited America over a hundred years ago.

He traveled from town to town, talking with people, asking questions and examining every facet of our society. Upon returning to France, he wrote these amazing words:

> "I sought for America's greatness. I found it not in her fields and forests. I found it not in her mines and factories. I found it not in her Congress and great tribunals. It was only when I entered her churches and heard her pulpits thundering against sin and preaching righteousness that I discovered the secret of her greatness … America is great because America is good. If America ever ceases to be good, America will cease to be great."

I don't blame our society or our government for the moral decay in our nation. I think the fault lies squarely with apathetic *Christians.* We have stood by and watched, refusing to leave the refuge of our pews to be salt and light in a decaying, dark culture. *Pathos* means, "to feel deeply." An a-pathetic Christian is someone who really doesn't care that our nation is in deep trouble. They don't even care enough to attend revival services, much less fast and pray for revival to come to our churches and our nation. Sadly, millions of Christians do not even vote in our local or national elections.

In 2 Chronicles 7:14, God addresses "My people" who are "called by my name." It's not up to the world to make a difference—it's up to *us*. The *only* way revival will come to America is when revival happens among God's people.

Two factors are *always* present in every great spiritual awakening: humility and prayer. Those aren't two separate steps; they happen simultaneously. The old evangelist Gypsy Smith used to say, "The way to revival is to draw a circle around yourself, get down on your knees and pray, 'Lord send a revival and let it begin inside this circle.'" The other requirement in 2 Chronicles 7:14 is to seek God's face and turn from sin. Those two steps happen simultaneously, too. What does it mean to seek God's face? When you come to God with a shopping list of requests, you seek God's *hand*. But when you come to God with surrender and submission, you are seeking His *face*.

When an ornate chapel was built at Versailles, the royal family sat in the center balcony opposite the altar. All the worshipers sat on the first floor *not* facing the priest or the altar but facing the king, with their backs turned to the altar. I'm afraid people still come to church and never seek God's face. Vance Havner once said of our nation, "The situation is desperate, but the saints are not." The word "repent" simply means to "turn away." It means we are walking in one direction, pursuing our own selfish desires, and we turn and walk in the opposite direction after God. There is HOPE for us as a nation if we are willing to turn away from sin and turn to God.

Having Only Positive Expectations

There is no secret or shortcut to revival. It happens as God prescribes. When you lower the temperature of water to 32 degrees, ice *will* form. It's just as certain that when we humble ourselves, pray, seek God's face and repent, God *will* hear from heaven, forgive our sin and heal our land. *We* can't heal America but *God* can. When we are faithful to do our part, He is *always* faithful to do His part and restore our HOPE again.